TRACK OF THE TIGER

LEGEND AND LORE OF THE GREAT CAT

EDITED BY MAURICE HORNOCKER

SIERRA CLUB BOOKS

A TEHABI BOOK

Stanley Breeden, an excerpt from "Tiger! Lord of the Indian Jungle," *National Geographic*, Vol. 166, No. 6, December 1984. Reprinted in this abridged form with permission by National Geographic Society.

Jim Corbett, "The Pipal Pani Tiger" excerpted from *Man-Eaters of Kumaon* by Jim Corbett. Oxford University Press, New York, 1946. Copyright © 1946 by Jim Corbett. Permission granted by Oxford University Press.

Peter Matthiessen, "Tiger in the Snow" first published in *The New Yorker*, January 6, 1997. Copyright © 1997 by Peter Matthiessen. Reprinted in this abridged form with permission by the author.

R. K. Narayan, an excerpt from *A Tiger for Malgudi*. William Heinemann Ltd., London. Copyright © 1983 by R. K. Narayan. Reprinted in this abridged form

with permission by Reed Books and the author.

Col. A. N. W. Powell, "Waiting and Watching" an excerpt from *Call of the Tiger* by A. N. W. Powell. A. S. Barnes and Company, New York, 1958. Copyright © 1958 by A. N. W. Powell. Reprinted with permission by Cornwall Books, New Jersey.

Elizabeth C. Reed, "White Tiger in My House," *National Geographic*, Vol. 137, No. 4, April 1970. Permission granted by National Geographic Society.

Geoffrey C. Ward, an excerpt from *Tiger-Wallahs—Encounters with the Men Who Tried to Save the Greatest of the Great Cats*. HarperCollins, New York, 1993. Copyright © 1993 by Geoffrey C. Ward with Diane Raines Ward. Reprinted in this abridged form with permission by the author and HarperCollins.

Library of Congress Cataloging-in-Publication Data
Track of the tiger : legend and lore of the great cat / edited by Maurice Hornocker
  p. cm.
"A Tehabi book."
ISBN 0-87156-973-6 (cloth: acid-free paper)
 1. Tigers 2. Tigers—Folklore 3. Tigers—Pictorial works.
 I. Hornocker, Maurice G.
QL737.C23T735 1997
599.756—dc21   97-19069
             CIP

Track of the Tiger was conceived and produced by Tehabi Books. http://www.tehabi.com
Nancy Cash–*Managing Editor;* Laura Georgakakos–*Manuscript Editor;* Anne Hayes–*Copy Proofer;* Sarah Morgans–*Editorial Assistant;* Sam Lewis–*Webmaster;* Andy Lewis–*Art Director;* Tom Lewis–*Editorial and Design Director;* Sharon Lewis–*Controller;* Chris Capen–*President.*

Sierra Club Books and Tehabi Books, in association with The Basic Foundation, a not-for-profit organization whose primary mission is reforestation, will facilitate the planting of two trees for every one tree used in the manufacture of this book. This edition is printed on acid-free paper that meets the American National Standards Institute z39.48 Standard.

For more information on Project Tiger and the Hornocker Wildlife Institute, write to P.O. Box 3246, University of Idaho, Moscow, Idaho, 83843.

Printed in Hong Kong through Dai Nippon. First edition 1997.   10 9 8 7 6 5 4 3 2 1

CONTENTS

NO PLACE LEFT TO HIDE

I SAW MY FIRST WILD TIGER IN India in the summer of 1971. The local tiger authority and I were crouched in a crumbling maharajah's shooting tower, listening more than watching in the stifling heat and mosquito-ridden darkness. Below us, the tethered water buffalo—tiger bait—stirred as it, too, sensed the tiger's approach. Then we heard him—a cough more than a roar. I'll never forget that sound. The powerful lights switched on and there he was, a mature male, startled but unafraid and almost defiant. For more than a half-minute he stood, seeking the source of this intrusion, then slowly, fluidly, he melted into the night.

That was in Sariska National Park in the state of Rajasthan, west of Delhi. A few days later in Uttar Pradesh, close to the Nepal border, I came close to my second tiger.

The famed tiger conservationist, Billy Singh, and I rode out on his faithful elephant to drive a tigress and her cubs from a sugar cane field. She had been attracted by the cool dampness under the impenetrable cane umbrella. But she was disrupting the harvest—workers were refusing to enter the field. As we approached the area where she last had been sighted, the old elephant stiffened under us, sensing the tiger's presence. But she then quickened her pace as though anticipating the encounter, plowing through the cane like a bulldozer behind the now-moving tigress. We never saw the tigress but, like the wise old elephant, we *sensed* her. It would be twenty-one years before I would see my next wild tiger—in the forest of Far Eastern Russia.

I was in India and Nepal for the Smithsonian

The tiger varies its hunting techniques based on the habits and activities of its prey.

Institution, attempting to determine the feasibility of a long-term research project on tigers. Eventually, my colleague and friend, John Seidensticker, would initiate that research in Nepal.

My interest in the great cats began with my work on the mountain lion in Idaho in the mid-1960s. Since that time, my colleagues, students, and I have conducted long-term research on all the North American cat species—mountain lion, lynx, bobcat, ocelot. My work has also taken me to the jaguar jungles of Central and South America and to the seat of everything biological—the leopard plains of Africa. Our leopard work of the 1970s remains a standard and one of my more satisfying efforts.

But I was never able to forget that male tiger in Sariska. The research I had helped initiate in Nepal was underway and Project Tiger had begun, so it wasn't as though the world was ignoring tigers. But that great tiger of the North—the world's largest cat—the great Siberian, remained a closed book. Behind the impenetrable Iron Curtain, the Siberian tiger existed, but that was all the rest of the world knew. I tried, in the mid-1970s, to visit the Amur region of Siberia by establishing contact with a Russian scientist in charge of a sanctuary where tiger sightings reportedly occurred. He was enthusiastic but Cold War bureaucratic bickering on both sides of the Pacific Ocean killed that opportunity before it had a real chance.

When President Nixon pried open the Chinese borders in the late 1970s, I seized the opportunity in 1980 to inspect tiger range in far northeast China. I came away disappointed and depressed because of the accelerating exploitation of the forests. It was obvious tigers in China would soon literally have no place to hide. Alas,

that has proven to be the case—only a handful of these splendid cats now exist in all of northeastern China.

So it was with great joy and expectation that I greeted the opportunity to study the great Siberian in his last real stronghold in Far Eastern Russia. My colleague, Howard Quigley, in 1989 first made contact with a visiting delegation from the powerful Soviet Academy of Sciences. The Soviet scientists enthusiastically encouraged us to visit and to arrange a cooperative research effort. We promptly followed up in the winter of 1989–90, visiting academy offices in Moscow and continuing on to the far east coast of Russia for a firsthand look at tiger range. Fund-raising efforts followed and on January 1, 1992, our team, consisting of Howard and Kathy Quigley, Dale Miquelle, and me, launched the first-ever intensive research effort, utilizing modern technology, on Siberian tigers. Our project, now in its sixth year, has been a joint undertaking and has been remarkably successful. We have hired Russian scientists, technicians, and students from the beginning, making it truly a Russian-American cooperative effort. Our research continues and promises to aid greatly in saving the great tigers of the snow.

Realistically, it will require more than sound biological and ecological knowledge to save the Siberian tiger, or any of the other four surviving tiger subspecies. Sound knowledge is the first and absolutely essential step in any conservation plan. But it will also take international resolve, plus consideration of all the political, economic, and cultural factors involved. It is a big order, but it must be achieved if tigers are to be saved.

We must convince local and regional authorities and citizens—with facts—that it is in their best interest to conserve rather than kill tigers. We must work with communities to develop realistic alternative economies at the same time utilizing the tiger as a conservation symbol. It follows that if the economy flourishes there is usually little political resistance to sound conservation practices.

Tigers have captured man's imagination since the beginning of time. The tiger's power, grace, and beauty have forever enthralled and inspired mankind and have achieved a cultural identity in some human societies. And cultural considerations can overpower both politics and economics. This may be the best hope for tigers in the long run. Just as cranes in Japan and cows in India (and Siberian tigers in native Siberian territory) transcend politics and economics, tigers throughout their range must do the same. We must now take the next step and work to elevate the tiger to such a status that it is absolutely unacceptable,

culturally, to kill a tiger anywhere.

That is where this book comes in—it will inspire readers and, hopefully, call them to action. No one can deny the absolute majesty of these creatures, and this stunning array of photographs depicts not only that unmatched beauty but the tiger's great athleticism as well. The authors are a diverse group—naturalists, hunters, writers, photographers, artists—and illustrate the broad spectrum of human culture enamored with this great cat. These authors, as evidenced by their years of interest with tigers, show that they care deeply about the survival of this species. If enough people *care,* worldwide, it is possible to provide for such magnificent creatures as tigers. It is my hope that this book will help toward this end.

When the air temperature gets hot, tigers do not go far from the water.

LENA

IN EARLY APRIL OF 1996, I went to the zoo in Indianapolis to pay my respects to a young Amur tiger, which I found stretched gracefully on a sunny ledge, the highest and most isolated point in an outside enclosure she shares with two other Amur tigers, another young female and an adult male. She peered at me—or, rather, past me, in the cat's indifferent manner—through the slanted ellipses of gold-amber eyes. Unlike her companions—and unlike most zoo tigers—this beautiful creature was born in the wild, and, as it happened, I had recently returned from southeastern Siberia, where I had visited the alder wood on a snowy ridge on which she had been captured four years earlier, an unweaned, orphaned cub.

According to her keepers, the young tigress remains rather shy and apprehensive around strangers, owing to the traumatic circumstances surrounding her capture; a young zoo-bred tigress, who is more gregarious, was placed in her enclosure as a "surrogate sibling," to help acclimate her to captivity and calm her down. The Siberian tigress is beautiful and healthy, at about two hundred and fifty pounds, and is exceptionally valuable because of her genes, which promise a welcome infusion of new blood into captive-tiger-breeding programs all over the country. This month, she is scheduled to be bred with a genetically suitable male from the Minnesota Zoo—one whose genes are not already widespread in American zoo populations. Her cubs would be exponentially more valuable in maintaining the small tiger population in the wild, but that is not her story. . . .

The tiger is a solitary animal. It is estimated that between twenty-five and thirty-five square miles is needed to support a single adult male.

In late June of 1992, I made my first visit to Primorski Krai, which curves south along the Sea of Japan like a great claw to its borders with northeastern China and North Korea. My destination was the Sikhote-Alin International Biosphere Reserve, the largest wildlife sanctuary in the Far East, consisting of a 1,350 square miles of forested mountains, clear silver torrents, and unbroken coast. Here the brown bear and lynx, wolf and salmon of the north share their range with the tiger and leopard and subtropical flycatchers in a remarkable faunal region, unlike any other wilderness on earth.

The Sikhote-Alin Mountains are the last stronghold of *Panthera tigris altaica*, the so-called Siberian, or Manchurian tiger, which as recently as the last century was common not only in Siberia but throughout northeastern China and the Korean Peninsula, and ranged west perhaps as far as Mongolia and Lake Baikal. Yet the heart of the tiger's range has always been the watershed of the mighty Amur River and its main tributary, the Ussuri, which form the eastern boundary of Russia and China. Known more precisely as the Amur tiger, it resembles the Indian, or Bengal, race in its general aspect, but there is more white in the striking patterns of the head and also on the underbelly, and the flame color is less intense—less fire orange than old gold. Although only slightly taller, the Amur race in its longhaired winter coat appears more massive than the Bengal—the only one of the five surviving tiger races or subspecies which compares to it in size—and captive males have approached a weight of a thousand pounds.

This largest of the earth's great cats is already effectively extinct in China and the Koreas, and the few hundred surviving in Russia were in mortal danger, when, in 1989, Russian tiger authorities and American wildlife biologists first discussed an international research program to study the ecology and range and habitat requirements of *P. t. altaica* as the basis for a comprehensive plan that would try to save it. In January of 1992, the Siberian Tiger Project was set up at Terney, a fishing port about two hundred miles northeast of Vladivostok, which is surrounded by the Sikhote-Alin Reserve. The American co-directors of the project, Dr. Maurice Hornocker and Dr. Howard Quigley, of the Hornocker Wildlife Institute, which is affiliated with the University of Idaho, were pioneers in the use of radio telemetry to conduct field studies of cougars and jaguars: after immobilizing the animal with drugs by means of a shotgun-fired dart, they would take its measurements and blood samples, then fit it with a radio collar that permitted scientists to monitor the animal's movements and arrive at a better understanding of its ecology and range.

I was eager to observe field operations, but, as it happened, I arrived two days too late to witness the capture and release of a large tigress nicknamed Lena, only the second study animal caught since the project had begun. At Terney, Hornocker, a rangy, well-weathered wildlife biologist in his early sixties, and a foremost authority on the great cats, introduced me to three of his associates: a husky young American, Dr. Dale Miquelle, and two of their Russian colleagues—Igor Nikolaiev and Evgeny Smirnov—who, before the arrival of radio telemetry, had done most of their extensive research by tracking the animals on foot in winter. The researchers told me that Lena's signals were still coming from a wooded drainage area known as the Kunalaika in the southern part of the reserve, very close to the site of her capture two days earlier. Though full recovery from the immobilization drug might take two or three days, they were concerned that Lena had not recovered faster and wandered farther.

The next day, in the hope of monitoring the tiger's signals more precisely, we trekked into the forest, following a creek upstream for several miles through hardwood taiga of oak and birch, cottonwood and maple, poplar, ash, and elm, with scattered pines. On a dim old trail, all but closed by ferns, were big, raw pugmarks, or footprints. Perhaps these had been made by Lena, perhaps not. Farther on were deep-scratched trees where a tiger had sharpened its claws. Eventually, we arrived at the site where Lena had been snared—a large cottonwood where the ground was torn up all around and a strong sapling as thick as a man's arm had been snapped off clean. Lena's captors spoke with quiet awe of the terrible roars and lunging, the ferocity, with which this young female had made three swift charges on the cable of her snare before Hornocker and Nikolaiev were able to tranquillize her with two darts. Since then, Lena had moved less than a mile upstream. Using some rough triangulation to fix her precise location, we paused at a point estimated by Hornocker to be approximately a hundred yards from the tiger. Over the receiver came more rapid beepings, indicating that Lena was up and moving and had us located, too. She did not roar, but nobody believed that she was in a good temper. I envisioned her with her head raised and alert, her small, round white-spotted ears twitching in the greenish sunlight. In the fragmented sun shafts of the woodland, the head would be camouflaged by bold black calligraphic lines inscribed on frost-bright brows and beard and ruff, in a beautiful and terrifying mask of snow and fire. . . .

In late summer, Dr. Hornocker wrote me to say that Lena had resumed hunting in a normal manner. Also, a third female had been snared and collared, and in October, in the northern part of the Sikhote-Alin, a fourth female and two half-grown cubs were caught, making six "marked" animals altogether. More exciting still was a discovery in the next month that Lena had produced a litter of four cubs. Elated, Hornocker suggested that I pay a return visit to Primorski Krai in winter, when I might hope to see a tiger in the snow. But in November he sent the terrible news that Dale Miquelle had found Lena's radio collar slashed from her neck and tossed into the snow. Apparently, she had been killed by poachers on a road edge. Of her cubs there was no sign whatsoever.

Because Lena had been the first "marked" animal to produce a litter, and was therefore of critical importance to many aspects of the tiger study, her loss was devastating. The heartbroken and enraged Miquelle had rushed back to Terney to report what had happened. Evgeny Smirnov and the reserve director, Anatoli Astafiev, accompanied by a forest guard and a police officer, returned with him to investigate the poaching site. While they were standing on the road, Smirnov glimpsed a movement in the bushes, and a moment later four tiger cubs were seen floundering uphill through the snow and alders. Though Miquelle tore off in pursuit, he was unable to catch them, yet it was clear that the unweaned and famished cubs, still awaiting their mother after a week or more, had kept circling back toward the killing place.

(Though only a few months old, they were already the size of bob-cats.) Realizing that they would not stray far, the men had returned to Terney and organized a capture party.

The next morning, the forest guard came upon two hiding cubs. Seizing one up against his chest and shouting for help, he stumbled along in pursuit of the other. By now, Astafiev and his party had come across the third and fourth, backed into a hollow tree. They were duly extricated, with precocious roars and snarling, and the capture of the four cubs left everyone in the party either scratched or bitten. Two of the cubs died of natural causes shortly after capture, but a month later, in January 1993, the two survivors were sent off on a five-thousand-mile journey to the United States, accompanied by Howard Quigley and his wife, Kathy, the project veterinarian. At the Omaha zoo, the cubs were placed in a captive-breeding program for endangered species, and a few months later one was transferred to Indianapolis, where the zoo staff, to commemorate her mother, named her Lena.

On January 18, 1996, when I returned to Primorski Krai, I was met at the Vladivostok airport by two of the wildlife biologists—Quigley, tall, trim-bearded, and soft-spoken, and the bearish Miquelle, now project field director. The Amur tiger, they told me, was more seriously endangered than ever. As a result of epidemic poaching, more than a third of the wild tigers were thought to have been destroyed since my last visit. Foreign enterprises—mining and timber interests in particular—had reportedly paid off officials for the right to ravage eastern Siberia. An assault on tiger country north of the reserve was under way, especially in the wild region of the Bikin River. However, neither Quigley nor Miquelle

had given up hope for the tiger, or lost enthusiasm for the project. At present, they said, the Sikhote-Alin Reserve was being used as a significant part of their territory by twenty to twenty-five tigers. Most of the tigers, however, lived outside the reserve, and they had to be given protection if the Amur race was to survive. Besides helping the local government improve public education about tigers, the project was encouraging the acquisition of wild land by the reserve and the establishment of woodland corridors between the scattered sanctuaries to allow young animals dispersing from a litter to encounter other tigers all the way south from the roadless region of the Bikin River to the Lazovsky Reserve, northeast of Vladivostok.

The following morning, we flew with Anatoli Astafiev up the icebound coast to a new timber-export facility at Plastun, and from there we continued north to Terney on the coast road. Terney, a village of small wooden houses painted zinc green or faded blue, of gardens and picket fences, outhouses, and trim wood-piles, and of twisting birch-shaded mud lanes climbing uphill and inland, looked much as it had on my first visit, but its seeming tranquillity disguised some disturbing changes. In Soviet days, guns and travel, not to speak of commerce, had been severely restricted—a circumstance that helped spare the beleaguered tigers. But, with the advent of capitalism and a free market, everything had been put up for sale, including the forests and their wildlife. Soon what had been iron borders were laid wide open to international trade, and local hunters turned poachers and smugglers made the most of their opportunity to supply tiger parts for traditional medicines to the Chinas and Koreas. The mainland

Chinese, in particular, were willing to pay as much as $10,000 for a single tiger—more than a local man might hope to make in five years' work—and were encouraging poaching in other tiger countries, especially India and Russia. They paid well not only for the beautiful striped pelt but for "medicine bones"—sinews, organs, glands, and even whiskers, which typically are ground to powder and consumed in the hope of curing mankind's afflictions, and also of acquiring the tiger's strength and its legendary potency, which permits it to mate vigorously over several days.

Thirteen tigers that had been collared and released since 1992 were being monitored biweekly from the air, and one morning, as the biplane used in project surveys crisscrossed an open valley and made a slow, grinding turn over a logging road, I saw the first wild tiger of my life, bounding swiftly across open ground through two feet of powder snow and whisking out of sight beneath a great lone spruce. Alerted, the pilot circled the spruce tighter and tighter. On that first sighting, with the low winter sun glancing off the snow, all I had seen was a leaping black silhouette, an emblematic tiger. (The image evoked a Tungus belief that stalking tigers use the sun to blind their prey, by springing out of the dawn light or the sunset like a spurt of flame.) But as the plane made a turn over the treetops, the tiger abandoned the lone tree and headed for a grove of pines nearby. I glimpsed a flash of bold color in the shifting greens, then the sunlit burnt orange and golden brown of a splendid creature moving purposefully but without haste over the snow; sheltered by the trees, it did not bound or hide but advanced unhurriedly down a sparkling white corridor between the pines.

The next day, with Quigley and Miquelle, I accompanied Anatoli Astafiev by car to the high-country logging village of Melnichnoye, where livelihoods were bound to be affected by a new western extension of the reserve.

At seven, the coast range was still locked in bitter darkness, and an hour later, though the sun had risen from the sea, the air remained transfixed by Arctic cold. At the Djigit River, a road led west over the mountains, following the southwestern boundary of the reserve in a gradual ascent into higher, colder country. Drab winter finches flitted across the white road and the ice-choked river like blown chips of bark, and a gray squirrel with handsome ear tassels cavorted up onto a snowbank and whisked down again. Twisting the bright orange cones among white snow caps on the fir tops was a flock of crossbills, the males fire red and black, the females a flame yellow.

On the four-hour journey there were no settlements, and the only traffic on the roads were the great logging trucks bound east from Melnichnoye to Plastun. In midmorning, we crossed a high divide and headed out across Sikhote-Alin's central plateaus, where the mountain air bit at the face like an ice tiger. Elk tracks wandered everywhere among snowy firs and bone white birches, and we chased from the roadside a young elk, woolly brown in its thick winter coat: it struggled away over a rocky knoll, up to its brisket in the snow. Farther on, Astafiev pointed with pride at mountain landmarks of the new reserve addition. Soon the road crossed the Kolumbey River, which traverses a high plain before descending west to the Ussuri. . . .

Before leaving Melnichnoye, we enjoyed a fine elk feast,

prepared by the local women, then returned to Terney, arriving about midnight. The following day, in the afternoon, we stopped again on the icebound empty road where Lena's collar had been found—not to commemorate Lena but because a tigress, Katia, which had taken over Lena's territory two years earlier and was thought to have cubs, had adopted Lena's troubling habit of hiding her litter in a den east of the road and crossing the road to hunt in the Kunalaika. Not fifty yards from where Lena had been killed—and this seemed eerie—we found Katia's tracks in the deep snow where she had come down the ridge and crossed the road to make her way to the elk bottoms. Her radio signal—a pulsing beat, like the hard chipping of a bird, or like the rubbing of two stones together—was loud and fast, but that might mean only that her collar was rubbing on a frozen kill.

To verify the existence of the litter, we wanted to check the tiger tracks around the kill. While Katia was present we could not go down there, for the sake of the tiger and her cubs as well as for our own sake. But that same evening, toward dusk, according to a reserve assistant, Alyosha Kostnya, Katia recrossed the road and climbed the eastern ridge, apparently on her way back to her litter. (As it turned out, she had just one cub, and she brought it across the road a few days later.) The following day, her signal, still coming from the east, indicated that she was resting, which is usual in the middle of the day, and so we descended through the hillside woods to find her kill.

The snow in the woods was two feet deep and fluffy with dry cold. In the deep frost, a pea green moth cocoon suspended from a twig was the solitary note of green. In the bottoms we followed the smooth white surface of the Kunalaika, which in this place might have been forty feet across. On the river ice, the snow left by the wind was light, and Katia's pugmarks were sharp, as if incised in steel. In one place, the tigress had lain down and stretched, leaving a ghostly outline . . . even to the great head and long tail, the leg crook, and the big, floppy paws—so clear that one could almost see the stripes.

Her ambush site was a river island of small, bent black saplings against snow—uncanny camouflage for the white accents of her mask and her vertical black markings. Not far away, the heart-shaped prints of a young elk broke the ice glaze on an oxbow off the river, and from the snow evidence we were able to reconstruct what had happened. The foreprints came together where the elk stopped short, in a place of elms and cottonwoods, some seventy yards from the crouched tiger. Perhaps the elk listened, sniffed, and trembled for a moment, big dark eyes round. From this taut point, it suddenly sprang sidewise, attaining the far bank in one scared bound, as the tigress launched herself from hiding and cut across her quarry's route in ten-foot leaps, leaving silent round explosions in the snow. Shooting through the dark riverine trees like a tongue of fire, she overtook the big deer and hauled it down in a wood of birch and poplar about thirty-seven yards (Miquelle paced it off) from where she'd started. Striking from behind, she'd grasped the throat, to suffocate her prey, for there was little blood—only the arcs of a bony elk leg sweeping weakly on the surface of the snow, and a last, sad spasm of the creature's urine.

With logging trucks howling past perhaps sixty yards up

the steep slope, this wood was much too close to the road. The tigress had dragged the elk some ninety yards farther back, across the oxbow and the swamp island to the western bank, where she had lain in hiding. . . . The elk's carcass was dropped beneath a thick-trunked alder with dry catkins. Here the tigress fed before moving the elk to a wiry thicket at the edge of a swampy meadow.

Of the elk, all that remained were the legs, the head, and the stiff, coarse hide, which are usually abandoned by the tiger. There was no meat left on the twisted carcass. The eyes were frozen to blue ice, too hard even for ravens. Nearby, along the dragging track were the tigress's redoubtable defecations, and Miquelle, delighted by what he called the clearest and most classic kill among a hundred-odd that he had seen, pointed out that she had hardly left her lair except to go relieve herself, which was why no detail of this ambush, kill, or feeding was obscured. "Can you imagine," he exclaimed, "what this place would look like if a human hunter had lived here for four days, coming and going!" Having seen this clear place in the winter forest, I understood much better how the Russian researchers, before the advent of radio telemetry here in Primorski Krai, had learned so much about *P. t. altaica* by reading the signs of life and death in the winter taiga. . . .

One cannot speak for those who live in tiger country, but, for my part, the spirit and the mystery of the tiger—merely knowing that he is there twitching his white brows in the snowing taiga—bring me deep happiness. That winter afternoon in the Kunalaika, the low sunlight in the south glancing off black silhouetted ridges and shattered into frozen blades by the black trees, the ringing clarity of the cat tracks on the ice, the blood trace and stark signs of the elk's passage—that was pure joy. As Howard Quigley once observed, "Life would be less without the tiger."

A *tiger stealthily approaches to within thirty to sixty feet of its prey and then waits, unmoving. It will not commit itself to movement until after the prey does.*

W*hen the prey makes its move to escape, the tiger attacks. With blinding speed, it explodes into a rush and, with carefully timed maneuvers, delivers a killing neck bite.*

Previous Page: **T**he gaping face grimace, known as the flehmen behavior, allows the tiger to increase its ability to smell by expanding the sensory organ above the palate. This behavior is exhibited by both male and female tigers at sites where other cats have marked their territory by spraying their scents.

Tiger cubs have a high mortality rate. Of one hundred tigers born, perhaps fifty live to the independent stage.

Many tigers are killed by poachers for their coats and for body parts which are prized for their supposed potency as medicines and aphrodisiacs.

TIGER-MAN

WHEN I TOLD RAMCHANDRAN, our guide at Sariska National Park, that my wife Diane and I were on our way to Ranthambhore with an introduction to its field director, Fateh Singh Rathore, he was clearly impressed. "A very dangerous man," he said, by which I think he meant that Fateh Singh was brave and resolute. He was in fact a legend among Indian conservationists: no wildlife official had worked harder or sacrificed more to protect the land and animals under his care; none had seen his hard work crowned with greater success.

Under his implacable protection, the number of tigers flourishing at Ranthambhore National Park had officially grown from thirteen to forty in just thirteen years. "You will see a tiger at Ranthambhore," Ramchandran assured me as I left Sariska. "Fateh Singh can *always* show you one."

Ranthambhore, located in the desert state of Rajasthan, at the junction of two ranges of red hills, the Vindhyas and Aravallis, is no more lush than Sariska: neon parakeets and iridescent bee-eaters provide the brightest spots of green among its seared hillsides. But it is far more beautiful. The towers and sprawling battlements of a vast, abandoned tenth-century fortress cover the top of its highest hill; for centuries, Ranthambhore was the hunting preserve of the princes of Jaipur, and scattered all through its forests are crumbling walls, fallen temples, and carved *chatris*—domed monuments, each marking the spot where some long-forgotten man of consequence was cremated.

Tigers have highly acute senses. Their hearing is as sharp as those of any animal, and their eyes are the brightest of any creature on earth.

A chain of three small, bright blue lakes runs down the center of the preserve. Crocodiles and soft-shelled turtles sun themselves and herds of chital browse along the shore. Sambar come down to the water, too, and splash right in to stay for hours, immersed among succulent lotus pads, their broad backs becoming islands for snowy egrets.

This extraordinary place was Fateh Singh's domain. He is a Rathore, a member of the ancient princely family of Jodhpur. He has none of his ancestors' bloody-mindedness, but he has inherited their fascination with the forest and their sense of proprietorship over everything that lives within it. To this day he speaks of Ranthambhore as "my park," its tigers as "my tigers"; and during our first visit with him, both did still seem to be his and his alone.

He was in his mid-forties then, short and chesty, with a steel gray mustache, and given to sporty hats, sunglasses, and dapper green safari clothes. There was little of the ascetic about him: he savored a bawdy joke and a stiff drink on the rooftop of his forest home after dark, and he let nothing interfere with his favorite situation comedy in Hindi, watched on a small black-and-white set powered by a car battery. But his animals came first, always; everything about them seemed to interest him.

"There's your music!" he shouted, as we drank a cup of tea shortly after dawn on our first morning at Ranthambhore. We were listening to the steady poot-poot-poot of the coppersmith, which, he said, meant that summer was coming fast. The forest chorus grew more complex, a discordant blending of the shrill triple-noted call of the gray partridge; the peacock's contralto *peeaor*; the insistent "Did-you-do-it? Did-you-do-it?" of the lap-

wing; finally, the gray langur monkeys' deep solemn hooting. "They're telling each other, 'I'm okay, you're okay,'" Fateh said. "Glad they got through another night."

Suddenly the langurs' mellow conversation turned to angry, hawking coughs. We put down our teacups and raced for Fateh's jeep. From their perches in the tops of trees, langurs are often the first to announce the presence of a prowling tiger. We would spend the next four days like firefighters, careening over the stony landscape to answer every alarm. As we drove, Fateh sat ramrod-stiff in the back, humming to himself at the sheer pleasure of being in his forest, and occasionally pointing out one or another of the 275 species of birds seen here.

Despite Ramchandran's confidence in him and Fateh Singh's intimate knowledge of the Ranthambhore tigers (half of which he knew by name and could identify at a glance), even he could not summon up a tiger to show visitors at will. We drove through his preserve for four days, off and on, listening for the alarm calls of deer and monkeys, and leaning down from time to time to examine the pugmarks of tigers that seemed always to have just preceded us on the twisting forest track.

In the late afternoons we parked overlooking one or another of the lakes, hoping to see a tiger charge out of the grass to kill one of the hundreds of deer feeding there. One evening as we sat watching in the fading golden light, we suddenly spotted two figures strolling along the path toward us: a tall Englishman hung with binoculars and wearing khaki shorts, arm-in-arm with an eighty-year-old Dutch woman whom I recognized as a fellow guest at the lakeside guesthouse called the Jogi Mahal. Just three days earlier, news had reached Ranthambhore that a tiger had killed another heedless Briton who had insisted on entering the forest on foot to get a closer look at a rare species of owl in the Corbett Tiger Reserve more than two days' drive to the north. Now this mismatched, oblivious couple had dawdled along for hundreds of yards between high yellow walls of grass whose soft sibilance in even a faint breeze can disguise the movements of the clumsiest tiger. Fateh was apoplectic. "Stupid! Stupid! Bloody idiots!" he shouted at the startled visitors, pulling them into his jeep. "I should throw you out of this park. You will get my tigers killed!"

People, not animals, remained his most vexing problem. In the heart of the Ranthambhore fortress is a temple dedicated to Ganesha, the fat, amiable, elephant-headed god who blesses all new ventures, including marriage and childbearing. Small groups of worshippers seeking his favor climb the hill every morning, and on one annual festival day some fifty thousand pilgrims troop along the main sanctuary road to converge on the temple. Even Fateh Singh did not dare interfere with the rights of the faithful to worship where they please, but he did worry about what might happen if one of his tigers should someday attack a pilgrim. (On the same festival day in 1988, Fateh's worst fears would be confirmed. A young tigress which had been prevented from crossing the road for hours by the parade of pilgrims streaming past without a break finally lashed out and killed a seven-year-old boy whose father had left him for a moment to relieve himself.)

Then, too, scattered among the deepest ravines, lived a handful of solitary sadhus—ascetic hermits who had vowed to end their days there, praying in the wilderness. Fateh wasn't sure how many there were—perhaps five, he said—and, so far, the animals had left them alone. The sadhus attributed this to the power of their own belief; Fateh credited "damned good luck."

He did the best he could to control the rest of those who sought admission to his sanctuary. No one was allowed to walk in the forest; tourists had to be driven by trained guards, and a good deal of his time was spent allocating seats for them among the small fleet of spavined vehicles at his disposal. One evening I counted thirty-nine spectators packed into five parked jeeps, all of us watching to see if a single noisy sambar calf would find its missing mother before a hungry predator found it. (It did.)

The most serious trouble came from local people. A dozen villages had been successfully shifted out of the park, but thirty more ringed its perimeter; its trees had always provided fuel for their cookfires; its grass and undergrowth had fed their herds; and the villagers were only bewildered and angered by the notion that the forest should suddenly be off-limits to them. Women slipped into the park through hidden ravines to cut the grass, carrying out great heaps of it on their heads. Troops of woodcutters entered, too, and so did herdsmen, and tribal hunters with packs of trained dogs.

Fateh Singh and his forest guards did their best to fend them all off, but it was not easy. He had too few men to patrol the entire border of the park. The grasscutters hid their curved blades beneath their skirts, then charged the guards with molestation when they were searched. When disputes arose, local politicians routinely favored the villagers—who can vote—over animals that cannot. . . .

His was an intensely personal struggle. Whenever he left his stronghold even for a few days, interlopers streamed across its borders and had to be driven out again when he got back. "It's an endless war," he told me as we drove through the forest on my last morning at Ranthambhore, and it was one he would have preferred not to have to fight. Despite almost daily threats and his own near-fatal beating, he refused to carry a gun—and wouldn't let his men carry them, either. "I'm too hot-tempered," he told me. "If I had a gun I know I would shoot someone." Besides, "we want to be friendly, to work *with* people, not against them. What we need is a 'Project People for Project Tiger.'" He called for teams of conservation workers to move from village to village, explaining the long-term benefits of keeping the forests intact; a program to recruit tribal hunters into the forest service so that their forest skills could be used to save animals rather than slaughter them. The periphery of the park should be replanted with improved grasses for harvesting, he said, but only to nourish stall-fed livestock—and funds had to be found to encourage traditional herdsmen to abandon their inferior, wasteful animals in favor of improved breeds. All of this would take time and money and coordinated planning.

In the meantime, the tigers of Ranthambhore had only Fateh Singh. He had worked within the sanctuary for nearly twenty years, and his success had several times led his superiors at Jaipur to promote him to a desk job. He always turned them down. He planned to stay in one place—and in charge—until he retired. "I know this place," he explained, rising in his seat to peek over the top of the thorn bushes. "I'm not happy anywhere else. I've bought myself a farm at the edge of the forest so that every day until I die I can drive over and visit my park."

He clutched my shoulder. "Tiger in the road," he said. Perhaps forty feet ahead of us a tiger sat in the middle of the track—filled the track, in fact, and seemed somehow to fill the forest that stretched away on either side as well. Nothing had prepared me for his size or for the palpable sense of menace and power that emanated from him. "His name is Akbar," Fateh whispered, beginning softly to hum with pleasure at the sight of him. "About five hundred pounds."

The tiger rose slowly to his feet. Everything about him seemed outsized: his big, round, ruffed face; his massive shoulders and blazing coat; his empty belly that hung in folds and had finally forced him into the open to hunt; his long twitching tail. It seemed inconceivable that such a big vivid animal could have stayed hidden in this drab open forest for so long.

We sat very still in the open jeep as the tiger stared at us. "He's a good boy," Fateh said, still humming. I devoutly hoped so. The tiger turned and cocked his huge head to listen as a sambar called from a clearing off to our left; then, after fixing us with one more steady glance, he slipped silently into the grass. Neither his smiling protector nor his protector's wary guests had been worth so much as a growl.

It is estimated that only one cub from each litter survives to maturity.

Tiger cubs are very playful and, like other higher mammals, have a distinct sense of fun.

EXCERPTED FROM A *NATIONAL GEOGRAPHIC* ARTICLE BY
ELIZABETH C. REED

THE FOSTER MOTHER

IT WASN'T MY HUSBAND'S fault. Still, the timing could not have been worse. I was busy in the kitchen, preparing dinner for fourteen guests, when he telephoned.

"Do you want the white cub now or later today?" Ted asked.

I should be used to that kind of question. My husband, Dr. Theodore H. Reed, directs the Smithsonian Institution's National Zoological Park in Washington, D.C. As a result, I've been foster mother to four hybrid bears, one grizzly cub, and two young leopards. Oh yes, and to a ring-tailed lemur that used to perch on my shoulder drinking orange juice.

Rewati, though, would be a different breed of cat—the only white tiger cub in the Americas. Ten years ago my husband had journeyed to India to escort her mother to this country. For the past decade, Mohini—Enchantress—has been one of the zoo's most popular attractions. With her blue eyes, and gray-brown stripes on whitish fur, Mohini is a mutant—a color variation of the orange Bengal tiger.

Zoo officials hoped to perpetuate Mohini's whiteness by mating her with Samson, an uncle of hers bred from an orange Bengal mother and a white father. In 1964 they were successful. Mohini gave birth to three cubs, including a white one, but the white cub died of a virus at nineteen months.

This time Mohini had been mated with another orange tiger carrying a white gene, Ramana, and eight days before my husband's telephone call she had

White tigers are rare occurences in nature.

given birth to a white female cub. Indian ambassador Nawab Ali Yavar Jung suggested her name, Rewati, after a pure mountain stream in his country.

Mohini had been a model mother at first, but now zoo officials were worried. She had begun to lick her offspring excessively and pace nervously around the cage carrying it in her mouth. The rare and valuable cub was in danger; someone would have to take over the mother's role.

My husband felt he had no right to ask any of his associates to assume that grave responsibility. Rewati would come to our house where he could watch her closely—and I was drafted as foster mother.

That afternoon, before the dinner party, Ted brought the baby tiger home. It was hard to realize, staring at that appealing little 2 1/2-pound bundle of fluff, that she would become a regal giant of four hundred pounds or more. We scurried around the house, turning an upstairs bedroom into a nursery, complete with incubator, baby scale, and nursing bottles.

If I was a bit preoccupied that night, I'm sure the guests understood. There was at least $10,000 worth of infant tiger in that incubator upstairs. And, really, it was more than just a matter of money. Countless thousands of people had already learned of Rewati through the news media, and were eager to see her when she was old enough to return to the zoo. What if I blundered in my mother's role? There was so much that I didn't know—that no one knew—about hand-raising a white tiger cub!

Of some three dozen white tigers in captivity, most remain in India. A pair in the Bristol Zoo in England has pro-duced four young; a female is owned by the Crandon Park Zoo in Miami. Mohini and her offspring complete the list of those living elsewhere.

Because the fat and protein content of nursing milk varies widely among the big cats, Ted had searched all available zoo literature for information on tiger's milk. He found nothing. We settled on a commercial formula for baby animals, and Rewati took an ounce of it. Well, the first hurdle was behind us; we would vary the formula cautiously, guided by the cub's growth rate and bowel movements.

My youngest child is eighteen, so I had forgotten how exhausting a new baby in the house can be. When Rewati began yowling her first night, Ted and I awoke with a start. Two pairs of bare feet hit the floor in unison. Arriving simultaneously, side by side, at the nursery doorway, we managed to wedge through—the way millions of other parents have done. Rewati just wanted her bottle and a dry blanket.

From that time on, she wanted those bottles every 3 1/2 hours around the clock. Soon, she would outgrow the incubator, graduate to an open box 2 1/2 by 4 feet, and then move on to a larger pen in the basement.

On the tenth day of her life—two days after she arrived at the house—both her blue eyes were open. On the thirteenth day she managed a wobbly walk. On the twenty-second day she exhibited signs of playfulness, shaking her towel like a puppy.

But her twenty-fourth day was the one I had been waiting for. Rewati slept the whole night through. And so did I.

Our first crisis came a few days later when we found the

cub crawling in tight circles, unable to use her hind legs. My husband consulted the zoo's veterinarian and other specialists. They treated Rewati without being sure what her ailment was. Rewati received antibiotics, oxygen treatments, outside exercise sessions, and a formula bolstered with egg and brandy. In a week she was well again, roaming our newly fenced backyard, which had now become her "jungle."

Her weight had tripled by then, and she had begun to feed from a bowl—baby cereal and strained beef mixed in milk. Frankly, Rewati was a messy eater; I faced a cleanup project after every meal.

A tigress grooms her cubs by licking them. I used a damp washrag on Rewati, and she'd roll her ice-blue eyes blissfully during the ceremony.

There was nothing catlike about the way she walked; her lunging, rolling gait, in fact, reminded me more of a puppy. She would prowl the dim recesses behind the shrubs, pausing now and then to sharpen her claws on my camellia bushes, then pounce out to attack the big red plastic ball that was her favorite toy.

Occasionally, we would let her roam free in the house. I still have vivid memories of cozy dinners—with a white tiger frolicking under the table.

One member of our family viewed Rewati's arrival with something less than enthusiasm—Ebony, our big black tomcat. In those early days, he'd stand in the nursery doorway glaring balefully while I attended to the tiny cub. Or was it a hungry glare? I kept the two apart.

But as the white cub grew, Ebony's attitude changed to one of aloofness. Rewati wanted to be friendly. She even sidled up to the cat and gave him a playful nuzzle. Ebony leaped up on the fence and sat there outraged, licking furiously at the spot where he had been "contaminated."

Until the tiger arrived, Ebony had taken our affection for granted. Now he felt that his place in the Reed household was threatened. At the slightest provocation, the tomcat would leap up on my lap, doing his best to play the role of a cuddly kitten.

Suddenly Ebony's troubles doubled. The zoo bought an orange Bengal cub as a playmate for Rewati. She was Sakhi—in Hindi, "close and dear companion."

The white cub and the orange one would romp in the yard together, much to Ebony's disgust. It was amusing to watch the tomcat prepare to traverse tiger country. He'd plot his course across the yard carefully—and I'm sure he had escape routes in mind every foot of the way.

Rewati hated to be alone. As long as someone was within sight when she was in the yard—even Ebony—she was content. If she was left alone, I could count on hearing yowls and a scratching on my kitchen door. "Spoiled tiger," appeared more than once in the record I kept on our tenant.

I tended to forget, sometimes, that everyone does not have a tiger in his house. One day a man from the electric company came by to read the meter. Preoccupied, I waved him toward the basement where Rewati was napping. The meterman survived the shock—though I did get a polite phone call from the electric company asking how long I planned to keep that tiger down there.

Like all proud parents, we invited friends to "come see

the baby," and they came by the dozens. I counted thirty-five adults and children in a single day. Ted brought fellow zoo officials home, too. He took one in to tiger-watch at midnight, and the stillness soon was shattered by tiger yowls. "Ted should let sleeping tigers lie" was my rather testy journal entry next day.

Sometimes, when Ted worked late, Rewati and I would watch television. The programs seemed a bit tame, though—with a white tiger curled up next to me on the couch.

She was my "$10,000 tiger." I managed to get used to that. Then Ted mentioned casually that she really was worth about $35,000 by now! I wished he hadn't told me.

I rarely left the house. But when it was absolutely necessary to go out, I'd round up a tiger-sitting friend and give her only one rule to follow. "If the house catches fire, just take the cub and leave."

By the sixtieth day, Rewati's weight had climbed to fifteen pounds and she was now eating ground meat. Even in play, her teeth and claws could hurt.

Before, it had been easy to get tiger-sitters when I had to leave the house for a few hours; now there was less enthusiasm.

The time had come to send Rewati to her permanent home in the zoo where Bert Barker, head keeper of the large carnivores, could assume the mother's role. Sakhi—three weeks younger than her white playmate—would stay on in the house for a couple of weeks until she was on a solid food diet. Then she too would become a zoo resident.

The two cubs had a final romp in our yard that last day. Even Ebony sensed something, for his icy reserve melted a bit. Crossing the yard, he stopped to eye a waving tiger tail. He couldn't resist; for a few seconds he batted the tail back and forth with his paws. Then, recovering his dignity, Ebony stalked off.

Rewati went home to the zoo, and two weeks later Sakhi left. My house has never seemed so large and quiet.

Do I miss my tigers? There were times—especially during those 3 A.M. feedings—when I'd mutter, "May this house be safe from tigers." But miss them? Of course I do.

It is comforting, though, to remember that both Rewati and Sakhi are secure and healthy under the tender care of Bert Barker. And neither of them will ever be lonely, for hundreds of thousands of adults and children visiting the zoo enjoy my tigers now.

And there's always this: One day my phone is sure to ring again, and Ted will be at the other end of the line, saying "Get the nursery ready."

I wonder what kind of infant I'll be asked to mother then? 🐾

A *tigress may first come into season when she is two and a half, and copulation may take place, but conception is not normally possible until the age of four.*

The number of cubs in a litter varies from one to five. Two or three cubs is probably most common.

Tigers generally lie up by day where there is a breeze and few flies and gnats, and mostly hunt by night.

A FAMILY AFFAIR

NOTHING IS MORE BORING or disappointing than to go out to a shooting block, and have to wait several days without news of a kill. I was once unlucky enough to find myself in this unfortunate position. Morning after morning the shikaris returned only to report that all baits were untouched, and I became heartily sick of seeing them shake their heads. And they, poor fellows, were as disappointed as myself. We had seen the tracks of a big tiger the morning after our arrival, and two days before that a tiger had killed the forest guard's best cow, less than half a mile from the forest bungalow. According to him, two tigers had fed and dragged the carcass about almost up to the very minute of my arrival. Since then baits had been tied out regularly every evening, but . . . *nothing!* As generally happens on such occasions, my shikaris began suspecting some evil spirit was at work, or there was some hoodoo in our midst, and, according to them, no tiger would touch the baits until this had been righted. The remedy suggested, of course, was the appeasement of the local deity by sacrificing a goat, but, when all the evidence had been fully discussed and thoroughly thrashed out, the blame really seemed to descend, not on any evil spirit, but on a poor wretched individual, who, on account of his local knowledge of the jungles, had been engaged as an assistant shikari. This poor unfortunate man had an implicit faith in the Will of the Creator. If ever anyone suggested that, perhaps, a bait had been tied out in the wrong place, he used to answer quite simply, "No, it is the will of God Almighty. If He ordains that a

Almost anything that moves in the jungle is potential prey. Abrupt movements trigger the attack reflex in tigers.

bait be taken, then only will it be taken." It was, of course, quite impossible to argue against anything like this, and, although I told him I did not think God would help us unless he took a little more trouble, and tied the baits a bit further away from home, he was still unconvinced, and his great faith remained unshaken.

My faith, however, had already suffered something of a setback. I felt something ought to be done, and, as exercise, and a little extra exertion often dispel doubts and superstitions, I told the head shikari, who used to enjoy an afternoon siesta, that he himself would have to go out that afternoon with the baits, and see that they were properly tied out as far out in the jungle as it was possible to go before nightfall. This was *not* a popular decision!

There is no truer saying than the one—"Man proposes, God disposes." The proposed jaunt into the jungle for the head shikari ended abruptly. Less than an hour after his departure, he and his men arrived back dripping with perspiration. They had just reached the place where a bait had always been tied, when a tiger roared a hundred yards ahead of them, and the whole party, as one man, together with the baits, had turned and fled. They said the tiger was still roaring, and asked me to go back with them. Fate had very neatly turned the tables on me!

On arrival at the spot, we soon discovered the fresh tracks of a tigress but, as she had ceased roaring, and entered dense jungle, it was impossible to locate her. We followed in the direction she had taken, and wasted considerable time hoping she would roar again, but she did not do so. The result of all this was that baits were tied out in exactly the same places as before!

At about midnight that night there was a terrific thun-

derstorm with torrential rain. It poured for four or five hours, and did not stop raining till dawn. When the shikaris went out in the morning, they found one of the baits had been taken. All tracks had been washed out by the rain, but the drag of the kill was still faintly visible, and, on following it up a short distance, the shikaris had seen two tigers on the kill. A big tiger, they said, had growled at them.

On hearing the news, I set out at once, but, no sooner had I got there than it started raining again. Actually this was more a help than a hindrance. The patter of the raindrops on the leaves enabled us to move noiselessly towards the kill. When we had got to about fifteen yards of it, the shikari suddenly pointed out a reddish object, under a bush, about ten yards to the right. Quite naturally, we concluded it was the tiger lying up near his kill, but although we could actually see the hair, we could not for the life of us make out what part of the tiger was showing. As I did not fancy hitting him in a soft spot as such close range, I signaled the shikari to pass me my field glasses. To my disgust it turned out to be a kakur (barking deer). We did not attempt to disturb him, but, presently, he got up, barked a couple of times and then went slowly up the hill. Strangely enough, I have quite often seen a kakur near a tiger kill, and, although I have never actually seen one eating from a kill, I rather suspect these small deer of being carnivorously inclined. Certainly a tame kakur will eat meat.

The half-eaten kill was lying on a level piece of ground at the foot of a hill. The only suitable tree for a machan was about twenty yards away, leaning over at a dangerous angle from the side of the hill towards the kill. Two thoughts struck me at once. Firstly, that a tiger could easily run up the tree trunk to share the machan with me and secondly, that it was a thin tree and might not stand the weight of my fifteen stone at the top end of it. But, as the jungle was quite unsuitable for a beat, there seemed no alternative but to sit up. I ordered the shikaris to get the machan ready, and also had the kill tied to a sapling, to prevent it from being dragged away.

I do not usually start sitting up till about four o'clock in the afternoon, but on this occasion I was half an hour early, because, after rain, tigers sometimes return early to their kills. When I had settled myself comfortably into my machan, I ordered my men to go away talking loudly. As usual, they shouted "*Chalo bhai*" (Come on brother) at the tops of their voices, and then coughed vigorously! Further words completely failed them. I have often wondered why men, who spend day and night talking nineteen to the dozen, become absolutely tongue-tied when ordered to talk! I have never yet been able to persuade shikaris to go away talking to each other in a normal way. Anyway, off they went, leaving me feeling anything but safe in my precarious machan.

It was a glorious afternoon. The rain clouds had disappeared and the sun was shining brightly. The leaves of the trees had been washed clean by the rain, and, instead of looking dusty and dull, they were now glistening and green. The whole jungle looked beautiful. I had been gazing into this lovely woodland for about ten minutes, when I heard something coming noisily down the hill behind me. I imagined it to be a troupe of monkeys. A

minute or two later, however, I caught a fleeting glimpse of a tiger, moving through the bushes towards the foot of my tree. Leaning over to have a good look, I discovered it was a cub, a bit bigger than a large Alsatian. It sat down right at the foot of my sloping tree! A minute later it was joined by another of about the same size. They were in a playful mood, and I wondered when they would start running up the tree trunk to start playing with me! Then they rolled over and over each other on the ground, and indulged in quite a fair amount of all-in wrestling, quite regardless of the noise they were making. I realized then that the noise I had mistaken for monkeys must have been these two playing on their way down the hill.

The game at the foot of the tree went on for a few minutes, and then one of the cubs, suddenly remembering the kill, broke away from his playmate, and stalked solemnly down the slope to the carcass. There he soon got down to business. Seizing bits of flesh with his teeth, he threw his full weight on to his haunches, jerking and tugging with all his might to tear off large lumps of meat from the carcass. The second cub sat watching him for a while, but shortly joined him in tearing at the kill. The two of them behaved like little savages over their meal, snarling and growling at each other, and competing for the best tidbits hidden inside the carcass. It was when both dived in together that the fiercest arguments took place. I was so engrossed watching this gruesome savagery, that I had not noticed the arrival of Mama, but there she was now, a fine big tigress, sitting up on her haunches, proudly watching her cubs fighting over their supper. All the same, she was very much on the alert, and kept looking all round, obviously doing sentry while the cubs were feeding. When, however, they had more or less finished their meal, she approached the kill, and, seizing it by the exposed rib with her teeth, lifted it off the ground, and tried to drag it away. But I had tied one of its legs to a sapling, and when she found she could not take it away, she, too, threw all her weight back on to her haunches, and gave the kill a couple of tremendous jerks, which would have snapped a single rope, but I had been careful to double this one! Strangely enough, this did not seem to raise any suspicions in her mind, though she did take the precaution to start feeding standing up to avoid all the stinging insects now teeming round the carcass. She too tore chunks of meat off the carcass, and gulped them down whole, and, by growling and snarling, kept the cubs away while she was eating. But, if by chance she tore off more than an easy mouthful, she used to carry it away in her mouth, and sit down a few yards away to chew and eat it there. Whenever she did this, the cubs seized the opportunity and returned hurriedly to the kill, to bite off as much as they possibly could during her absence.

What worried me now was that a whole liver weighing several pounds was lying a few feet away from the kill, but neither the tigress nor the cubs had noticed it. I kept wondering how long this juicy morsel would remain undiscovered, and which of the three would be the lucky one to find it. When, however, the tigress had more or less satisfied her hunger, and had given up making quite such vigorous tugs at the kill, the liver caught her eye, and, after bending down to sniff it, she picked it up in her mouth, gave it a couple of hearty chews, and swallowed the whole thing in one big gulp. This then was the savoury! Looking well pleased with herself, the tigress now stalked off and sat down about ten yards away. Actually, she had not taken more than about ten minutes over her dinner, and now the cubs were down to business again, tugging away as hard as they could at the carcass. Occasionally they stopped, and one or other of them would walk over to the tigress, who, from time to time, growled, purred, made a sort of throaty hissing sound, and twice made a chirruping-whistling noise, which I had never heard before.

Just before dusk, with the tigress and cubs still lying about near the kill, I was delighted to hear the full-throated roar of a tiger about half a mile away. Surely, this was Papa, coming along to have his dinner. For the first time now my thoughts flew to my rifle. But when the tigress heard the roar she sprang to her feet immediately, and the two cubs at once dashed to her side. In absolute silence, they stood looking in the direction of the roar. When the tiger roared again, the tigress's body literally heaved as she tried to suppress an answering roar. She was obviously dying to answer the tiger, but her motherly instinct made her refrain from doing so. The tiger, still roaring, went down the forest road about a furlong away, but did not come to the kill, and I firmly believe he did not know anything about it. He, however, put the wind up my shikaris who were waiting further down the road. Needless to say they had all climbed trees, and stayed in them till the danger had gone by!

When it got dark it was up to me to obey the forest rule, and get down from my tree to go home, but, with the tigress and cubs still having occasional tugs at the kill, I wondered how this was to be accomplished. They had been with me now for over three hours, and much as I had enjoyed their company, it was now time to call it a day. I therefore began trying to pave the way for my departure. First of all I flashed my torch on the kill. The tigress immediately bolted. Both cubs were on the kill. One was buried head and shoulders inside the carcass, so he did not notice the bright light, but the other had obviously never seen such a thing before, and, after staring and blinking at the light, turned right round and began displaying the keenest interest in its own shadow. This was most unexpected, and I had great fun shaking the torch, and making the cub jump after its shadow. Eventually, both cubs sat together watching their shadows, but it did not seem to strike either of them that they themselves were being watched by anyone. Next I blew my whistle, which was the signal for the shikaris to come and fetch me down, but although they heard me and shouted to say they were coming, the cubs still sat on. Realizing that it would be serious if the tigress came back to protect them, I clapped my hands several times, but still with no result. As the shikaris now were only a couple of hundred yards away, I shouted to them to halt, but it was not until I had shouted again at the cubs, that they finally decided to move slowly away.

When I got down from my machan and told the story, the shikaris were most disappointed I had not shot the tigress, and I am afraid no argument would have convinced them that I had acted rightly in sparing her life. It had been lucky for her that her cubs came to the kill before her, or things might have turned out otherwise, and I should have lost three hours of interesting jungle entertainment.

It had been interesting to see how the tigress and her cubs behaved when they heard a male tiger roaring. It is generally accepted that a big male tiger will kill a small male cub if he comes across it. A tigress therefore takes good care to keep her cubs out of Papa's way while they are young. Actually, she always separates from her mate before the cubs are born, and goes away to some remote jungle, as far away as possible from the beats of all other tigers. This is done primarily to avoid the notoriously bad temper of her spouse, who is intolerant while the cubs are young and at the silly stage. Later, when they are well grown and have learnt how to behave properly, they return with their mother to her old haunts, and sometimes even rejoin Father, who then does not take exception to his well-behaved children. It may even be considered a pity that this system is not more universally adopted! It is not uncommon to come across tiger families of Papa, Mama, and two or three cubs, all living happily together, but this does not happen until the cubs have reached the age of reason.

I cannot describe what infinite pleasure it gave me to see these two cubs, the tigers of tomorrow, at home in the jungle with their mother. I wished over and over again that I had had a camera with me in my machan.

Tigers keep all four feet on or close to the ground as long as possible before attacking. They typically sight a victim and then stalk through cover to get close enough to rush.

It is possible to distinguish the pugmarks of a male, which are squarer and have thicker toes, from those of a female. Pugmarks can also indicate age, as well as the weight and size of a cat, which can be approximated from the depth of the indentation.

AN ORIGINAL ESSAY BY

MAURICE HORNOCKER

A CHANCE FOR SURVIVAL

IGOR NIKOLAIEV TURNED IN the trail and, without speaking, warned us to proceed quietly. His face, weathered by decades of Siberian winters, showed his anxiety and concern. He stopped near the deep forest's edge and, raising his arm, indicated where the snared tigress was concealed in the tall meadow grass. As he did so, without warning, the huge tigress erupted from cover barely yards away with a roar that literally shook the earth. Plunging toward us with another deafening roar, she was stopped short by the cable firmly gripping her left front paw. Snapped back to attention by the fallen tigress, the three of us—Igor, Dale Miquelle, and me—split up and circled her, looking for any opportunity to fire our tranquilizing guns. Twice more she made those heart-stopping lunges, each time her roars louder and more frightening. Hearts pounding, we edged closer and almost simultaneously, from opposite sides, Dale and I fired our tranquilizing darts. . . .

In order to study secretive species like tigers, we must observe them indirectly—direct observation is impossible. We do this by utilizing radio-telemetry. Each tiger must be captured and a collar carrying a small transmitter placed on its neck. Each tiger would have a transmitter sending an identifying signal. By monitoring each individual from season to season throughout the year, and from year to year, we gain the required information on individuals and on the entire population. We would prefer not to capture a single tiger, but there is simply no other way. The brief period of discomfort the individual endures seems a small price

An old tiger is threatened by starvation as its hunting ability wanes, and by attacks from younger tigers against which it can no longer defend itself.

to pay for information that can save the species. The alternative is to do nothing and watch, helpless without sound information, as this magnificent animal accelerates toward extinction.

The first step had been capturing the tiger. We first tried huge box traps, without success—the tigers either ignored or avoided them. We then suggested to our Russian colleagues using cable foot snares. This most humane device had been developed for capturing bears and had been in use for decades. Unlike some leg-hold devices, which close with much force, the cable snare merely tightens on the sinewy paw. Injuries to captured animals are practically nonexistent. We used them with great success on mountain lions in New Mexico, the first big cats to be captured with this device. Our Russian colleagues agreed to their use, and in February 1992 Howard and Kathy Quigley and Dale Miquelle, along with Igor Nikolaiev and Evgeny Smirnov, captured—for the first time ever—a Siberian tiger in such a cable snare. It was now June and we had our second capture—the big, snared tigress glaring at us from her partial concealment in the emerald meadow grass. . . .

The tigress snapped at the tranquilizer-laden dart as it struck her muscular shoulder. But she was too intent on us to persist in tending to this mere bee-sting sensation. Gradually she relaxed as the drug took effect, and after about three minutes she gently eased to her belly in the long grass. A minute more and she lowered her head in a restful position. She was now tranquilized, resting peacefully.

We approached her cautiously nonetheless, testing her responsiveness with a long stick. Satisfied she was safe to process, we began the task at hand—attaching the radio collar, taking weight and body measurements and withdrawing blood samples for later analysis and genetic testing. The research team's movements and intensity are not unlike those of a pit crew at a car race—accomplish the required tasks as quickly and cleanly as possible to allow a minimum of delay in sending the subject back on its way. Through the whole process (which lasted only fifteen minutes) I could only marvel at her beauty and awesome physical presence. I had handled many species of big cats during my thirty-five-year career, but none so impressive as this largest of all the world's cats.

We finished our work and withdrew a half mile away or so to await her recovery. Within the hour her radio signal indicated she was up and moving slowly up the drainage.

We named her Lena and with this successful marking I felt we were on our way to obtaining solid, useful data that could save the species. Since that morning in June 1992, we have placed radio collars on fifteen more tigers. From monitoring these tigers—some for more than five years now—we have built a sound foundation of biological knowledge about Siberian tigers. We know how much space they require, what they eat, how often they breed, what becomes of the young, how they react to man's activities, and what makes for good tiger habitat. In other words, we now have the information that can save the Siberian tiger from extinction.

Using this information and working with our Russian colleagues, we submitted a tiger habitat protection plan to the Russian Ministry of the Environment in Moscow and it was adopted as part of their government's official tiger conservation grand plan. Working with Dr. Astafiev at the Sikhote-Alin International Biosphere

Reserve, we helped implement his plan to expand the reserve to incorporate critical tiger habitat, an expansion so large it could be compared to enlarging Yellowstone National Park by 20 percent to provide for grizzly bears or bison. We secured the funding in the United States to accomplish this.*

It is fact, however, that any conservation program, anywhere in the world, requires attention to more than just biology. A successful conservation program must consider economics, politics, and the human culture. We have initiated a large-scale project on community development and alternative economies, utilizing the forest in a sustained manner. The utilization of sustainable forest products such as berries, nuts, mushrooms, ginseng, and wild honey once flourished in many communities. We are working with community leaders to revive many of these economically viable cottage industries. Such practices can enhance a forest ecosystem for both tigers and their prey while providing for the people.

From the beginning, we have attempted to address all these factors. But before we could be effective, we had to gain credibility. We did this by hard work and a spirit of cooperation. We hired the three top Russian scientists and aides; we provided for Russian student participation, working with their advisors at the University of Moscow. We created a truly cooperative effort at the local and regional levels. We not only worked alongside our Russian colleagues on a daily basis, but we bought property, when it became possible to do so, and moved into neighborhoods in the village of Terney, close to the tiger preserve. In other words, we literally became part of the community. All this convinced our Russian cohorts and neighbors that we were committed. And *commitment*

is crucial, along with scientific credibility, in selling a long-term program of conservation.

The number of tigers was extremely low when the Sikhote-Alin Biosphere Reserve was established in 1936—some estimate only about fifty individuals. The establishment of this reserve is regarded by many Russians as the most important factor in preventing the Siberian tiger (also called the Amur tiger) from going extinct. Once plentiful throughout Siberia, from Lake Baikal east to the coast and south into China and Korea, it now occurs in numbers only in this area of far eastern Russia. Hunted relentlessly for its skin and body parts—important in Asian folk medicine—the tiger has disappeared from most of its former range. Ironically, it began a recovery under Communist rule. Borders were closed to trade and poaching was not a problem. There was no economic incentive to cut the forests, so the tigers' habitat remained intact. And the forests were managed carefully to provide for wild boar, red deer, and other food species for man—food species for tigers as well. By 1985 there were an estimated 450 tigers in the Sikhote-Alin, a remarkable comeback.

This was encouraging to everyone we talked with on our first visit in 1990, but the scientists all cautioned that 450 still really were not very many. Little did we suspect then that this was so true and that scarcely two years later, with the dissolution of the Soviet Union and the opening of its borders, tigers would again be under siege.

It is absolutely essential that local and regional people be convinced it is in their best interest to conserve rather than kill tigers. But there must be a viable economy in place that sustains rather than destroys the forest. Political direction is usually dictated by economic direction and if we can bring about favorable economic development—favorable to the forest and to tigers—then politics and politicians will be on our side.

Cultural factors can be powerful forces in conservation, sometimes more powerful than economic or political concerns. There are examples from old cultures—sacred cows in India, cranes in Japan, tigers to the native Siberian Udege people—and some more recent examples. Birds of prey, considered vermin in rural North America since European settlement, are now protected and have become symbols of conservation success. Even sharks are shedding their evil image in many circles. Big carnivores like wolves and mountain lions are held inviolate and are admired by millions. Grizzly bears, once limited to restricted areas in national parks, are being considered for reintroduction into their historic range.

We are making an effort to promote tigers as such symbols and such superb creatures that it would be culturally unacceptable to kill them anywhere, for any reason. This step requires education at all levels and not only where tigers live, but internationally as well. We are working with elementary school teachers in Terney and other communities to bring awareness to Russian youngsters. Kathy Quigley, the project veterinarian, coordinated an art exchange between students in Terney and Moscow, Idaho, (location of the Hornocker Wildlife Institute). Views of the tiger by children on both sides of the world were surprisingly similar and positive. We are providing materials to the media throughout tiger range to promote understanding and conservation. We distribute calendars and posters imploring people to respect the tiger. These

items are tremendously popular and some have even become items of local trade. We write articles for the international media and produce films, all aimed at bringing international attention to tiger conservation.

These are problems that must be addressed and solved now, before it is too late. Poaching became a serious threat immediately after the borders opened after the fall of Communism. Some experts estimate that 100 to 150 of the 400 or so Siberian tigers in existence were killed the first two years. There is good news here—antipoaching teams have reduced poaching dramatically. Forest destruction must also be stopped. That does not mean stopping utilization of the forest—it means stopping destructive practices. If the forest is used properly, it can even benefit and improve standards of living for local and regional people and provide for tigers as well. Early on we coined the slogan "Save the Taiga, Save the Tiger." If we can save the forest, we can save the tiger.

Our work continues and we have high hopes we can save this great tiger, the biggest and most majestic of all the tigers. Some of the other subspecies farther south may be hopelessly overwhelmed by human populations in the not-too-distant future. But the great Siberian may—can—survive. It lives in a region of the world which is thinly populated with humans, the habitat is still largely intact, and the Russian people truly do want to save it. Of all the tiger species, this one has the best chance of survival. Evidence for this is results of the latest snow census, taken in February 1996, which showed a population of 350 adults accompanied by 101 cubs or subadults. This is most encouraging and confirms that our efforts are yielding positive results.

On a bright January afternoon, my friend "Dema" Pikunov

and I sat back on an outcrop overlooking the pristine coastal forest. He, Igor Nikolaiev, and two friends had invited me to accompany them on a wild boar hunt deep in the taiga, far from human habitation. As we munched hard Russian bread and deer jerky, Dema, an outspoken critic of any exploitation of his forest, lamented the recent loss of resources held so dear by both native people and generations of Russians. To him, a healthy forest means healthy people, both mentally and physically. He likens destructive logging practices to "cutting off the limb we're sitting on"— that life in far eastern Russia as he has known and enjoyed it will end if such practices continue.

I could not agree more with him and thought of similar situations in my own country. Dema's thoughts and my own tend to strengthen our resolve to work harder to make the difference. Our group of committed Russian and American scientists, passionate in their resolve, are doing just that. By utilizing the tiger as a conservation symbol, we hope to literally save entire ecosystems for the benefit of tigers, their prey, and the human societies living there.

The courageous late Mollie Beattie, director of the U.S. Fish and Wildlife Service, told journalist Peter Jennings in her last interview that one of her greatest fears was that children today might never be able to see a wild tiger. Unless we, she added, make the difference. Today, we and our Russian colleagues are working to make that difference, to secure a place for the great tiger in our children's tomorrow.

The Hornocker Wildlife Institute acknowledges financial support from the National Geographic Society, National Fish and Wildlife Foundation, National Wildlife Federation, Exxon, Richard King Mellon Foundation, and Liz Claiborne/Art Ortenberg Foundation.

Tigers will hunt for fish or any animal that lives along the river bank.

During the day tigers move through cover, stepping out at vantage points to scan and listen.

R. K. NARAYAN

THE TIGER'S TALE

I HAVE NO IDEA OF THE EXTENT of this zoo. I know only my corner and whatever passes before me. On the day I was wheeled in, I only noticed two gates opening to admit me. When I stood up I caught a glimpse of some cages ahead and also heard the voice of a lion. The man who had transferred me from the forest stepped out of his jeep and said after a glance in my direction, "He is all right. Now run up and see if the end cage is ready. . . ."

Men, women, and children peer through the bars, and sometimes cry aloud, "Ah, see this tiger. What a ferocious beast!" and make crude noises to rouse me, fling a stone if the keeper is not looking, and move on to appreciate similarly the occupant of the next cage. You are not likely to understand that I am different from the tiger next door, that I possess a soul within this forbidding exterior. I can think, analyze, judge, remember and do everything that you do, perhaps with greater subtlety and sense. I lack only the faculty of speech.

But if you could read my thoughts, you would be welcome to come in and listen to the story of my life. At least, you could slip your arm through the bars and touch me and I will hold out my forepaw to greet you, after retracting my claws, of course. You are carried away by appearances—my claws and fangs and the glowing eyes frighten you no doubt. I don't blame you. I don't know why God has chosen to give us this fierce make-up, the same God who has created the parrot, the peacock, and the deer, which inspire poets

Males use moans and roars of varying intensity, particularly at a kill site, to avoid encounters with other tigers.

and painters. I would not blame you for keeping your distance—I myself shudder at my own reflection on the still surface of a pond while crouching for a drink of water. . . .

I recollect my early days as a cave-dweller and jungle beast . . . with a mixture of pleasure and shame. At the far end of Mempi range, which trails off into the plains, I lived in my cave on the edge of a little rivulet, which swelled and roared along when it rained in the hills but was fordable in dry season, with the jungle stretching away on the other side. I remember my cubhood when I frolicked on the sandy bank and in the cool stream, protected and fed by a mother. I had no doubt whatever that she would live forever to look after me: a natural delusion which afflicts all creatures, including human beings. However, she just vanished from my world one evening. I was seized with panic and hid myself in the cave. When I ventured out, I was chased, knocked down and hurt by bigger animals and menaced by lesser ones. I starved except when I could catch miserable creatures such as rabbits, foxcubs, and squirrrels, and survived somehow. Not only survived, but in the course of time considered myself the Supreme Lord of the Jungle, afraid of no one, striking terror in others. It was, naturally, a time of utter wildness, violence, and unthinking cruelty inflicted on weaker creatures. Everyone I encountered proved weaker and submissive, but that submissiveness did not count—I delivered the fatal blow in any case when I wished and strode about as the King of the Forest. By the way, who crowned the lion King of the Forest? Probably a fable-writer, carried away by the pompous mane and beard, I suppose! A more slothful creature was never created. All his energy is conserved for hunting food, and once that is accomplished he lies down for days on end, so reluctant to move a muscle that he could be used by any other jungle creature as a mattress; it would make no difference to him if birds nested in his beard and laid eggs. As for his supreme strength I had a chance to test it in the circus ring once, when we were let out to fight and he fled into a waiting cage thanking the Creator for the damage of only one ear, which came off when I tried to comb his royal mane. I got a pat on my back from the ringmaster himself.

Every creature in the jungle trembled when it sensed my approach. "Let them tremble and understand who is the Master, Lord of this world," I thought with pride. When I strode out from the cave, the scent went ahead, and except monkeys and birds on trees all other creatures shrank out of sight. While I prowled through, half-sunk in jungle grass, I expected the deferential withdrawal from my path of other creatures. We the denizens of the jungle can communicate, without words, exactly as human beings do—we are capable of expressing to each other sympathy, warning, abuse, irony, insult, love, and hatred exactly in the manner of human beings, but only when necessary unlike human beings who talk all their waking hours, and even in sleep. When I passed by, rabbits scurried off, and if a jackal happened to be in my path, he put his ears back, lowered his tail, rolled his eyes in humility, and cried softly: "Here comes our Lord and Master. Keep his path clear . . ." Such attention pleased me, and seemed to add to my stature. Occasionally I came across a recalcitrant member of our society who probably thought highly of himself and I always noted, through a corner of my eye, how he pretended not to have seen me, looking the other way or asleep behind a thorny bush out of my reach. I made a mental note of such lapses of courtesy and never failed to punish him when a chance occurred. It might not be more than a scratch or a bite while passing him the next time, but that would take days to heal, and he would lose an eye or a tooth or earn a cut on his lips making it impossible for him to eat his food, all of which I counted as a trophy. Whenever I saw the creature again, you may be sure he never displayed any arrogance. Among our jungle community, we had an understanding, which was an acknowledgement of my superiority, unquestioned, undisputed. . . .

Forgive me, if you find me running into the past. When I recollect my forest life, I am likely to lose all restraint. . . .

I only worried about monkeys—they lived at a height and moved and ran about as they pleased, and thought they were above the normal rules and laws of the jungle, a mischievous tribe. I was aware of how they hopped from place to place, hiding amidst foliage, bearing malicious rumours and trying to damage my authority. Their allies were birds which lived at a height and enjoyed greater facility than monkeys in that they could fly away at my approach. How I longed sometimes to be able to climb or fly even a short distance. Then I would have eliminated this whole contemptible clan; I particularly wished to get at the owl, the wise one with his round eyes always looking down his hook nose, a self-appointed adviser to all those despicable creatures who secretly wished my downfall. (I'm only expressing my mentality in those days in the idiom of those times.) Every time I passed below a tree, I would hear a cynical cackle and hoot and if I looked up I'd see the loving couple, the owl and her mate. One would say to the other, "When the King passes, what should one do?" There

would be some answer to that.

"If you don't?"

"Then he will nip off your head."

"Yes—only if he could carry his mighty bulk up a tree trunk . . ."

The crow was particularly treacherous, always following my movements and creating enough din to reveal where I had the kill, making it impossible for me to eat in peace, sneaking up to peck at my food and retreating when I turned, again and again. Worse than the crow were kites, vultures, eagles and such, which circled loftily in the high heaven, but to no greater purpose than to spot carrion, glide down and clean it up to the bone. Mean creatures, ever on the watch for someone else's kill.

Another creature that I had my eyes on was the leopard. I don't know how many members of that odious family existed in my forest—they didn't seem to breed or multiply too openly. The leopard was so secretive that you never noticed more than one at a time and hardly ever a family. It has always been a mystery. When I passed by he would climb a tree pointedly to emphasize the fact that he was higher than myself. I tried to ignore this creature, since he possessed great agility and could get beyond anyone's reach, but he was mean, and always made it clear that he was there and didn't care for me. He made all kinds of noises while I passed, and purred and growled and sneered. When he was with his mate it was worse. They made audible remarks most insulting to a tiger, and talked among themselves about the superiority of spots over stripes.

There was a jungle superstition about how the tiger came

to have stripes. The first tiger in creation was very much like a lion, endowed with a tawny, shining coat of pure gold. Imagine! But he offended some forest spirit, which branded his back with hot coal. Thus goes the fable, which I didn't believe in, a canard started by some jealous creature like the leopard who felt inferior owing to his spots, but made a virtue of it. The leopard couple sang this fable every time I passed by, a monotonous silly song; I would have put an end to their song if I could have seen where they were—they were mostly unseen, and just streaked away like lightning when glimpsed. I was helpless with this truant. It hurt my pride as a ruler of the jungle, while all other creatures respected my status, bowed to it and kept out of my way. Night and day I spent in planning and thinking how best to humble the leopard or exterminate him. Sometimes I set out to track him down in his lair, in a deep hollow or inside a cave. When I went in quest, he would invariably anticipate my arrival and sneak away, and then sit atop a steep, slippery rock, and eye me with contempt or go up a banyan tree with the ease of a squirrel . . . I realized soon that I had to tolerate his existence and bide my time. This was a great worry for me. He disturbed and scared off my game and was ahead of me in hunting.

The leopard was not the last of my worries. I could ignore him and go my way. Not so a female of our species, whom I encountered beyond those mango groves—a creature as large as myself, I suppose. I smelt her presence a long way off. I hesitated whether to turn back or advance. I was out to hunt for the evening, and if I had not been hungry I would have withdrawn and gone my way in a different direction. But I was proceeding to the meadow beyond the valley where I knew a herd of deer always grazed. I noticed her sitting erect in the middle of the road blocking my passage. I'd never seen her before; probably from an adjoining forest. Normally we respected each other's territories and never intruded. My temper rose at the sight of her. "Get out of my way and go back where you belong," I roared. She just took it as a joke and showed no response except a slight wave of her tail. This was complete insolence and not to be tolerated. With her back to me she was watching the herd in the meadow. I was furious and jumped on her back and tried to throttle her, with the sort of hold that would make a wild buffalo limp in a second. But this lady surprised me by throwing me off her back with a jerk. My claws were buried in her skin, but that did not make any difference to her as she turned round and gashed my eyes and bit my throat. Fortunately I had shut my eyes, but my brow was torn and blood trickled down my eyes. The jackal, as always attracted by the smell of blood, was there as if summoned, hiding behind a thicket of thorns; he made his presence felt, and mumbled some advice, which was lost in the uproar the lady was creating as she returned for the attack and knocked me off my feet by ramming into me. I have never encountered anyone so strong. Now the safest course for me would be to retreat gracefully to my cave and get away from this monster quickly. But my dignity would be lost—especially with the jackal there watching my humiliation. I should fight it out, even if one of us were to die in the process. We butted into each other, scratched, clawed, wrestled, grappled, gashing, biting, tearing each other, and I also stood up and threw my weight on her and struck, but it was like beating a rock—she was no normal animal: there is a limit to physical endurance; and I could stand it no longer; I collapsed on the ground bleeding from every pore; I had no strength even to run away, which I wished I had done earlier instead of bothering about prestige before the damned jackal. If I had seized and choked the jackal, I could have saved my blood.

In a few places my skin hung down in ribbons. My satisfaction was that the monster, my adversary, seemed to have fared no better. She had also collapsed in a ditch, no less bloody, with her flesh torn up and exposed. I noticed also that while I could open my eyes with blood dripping, she lay with her eyes swollen and sealed. I remembered aiming at her eyes just as she was trying to gouge out mine, but I seemed to have had better luck. It was her inability to open her eyes, more than physical collapse, which forced her to withdraw.

While both of us lay panting, the jackal came out of his shelter and, standing at a safe distance, raised his voice so that both of us could hear him. He knew that neither of us was in a state to go for him if we did not like his words; all the same he kept his distance and a possible retreat open. The jackal asked with an air of great humility, "May I know why you have been fighting and brought on yourselves this misery? If you can show even half of half a reason, I shall be satisfied." Neither of us could answer, but only moan and growl. For the condition I was in, the jackal could have patted my cheeks or pulled my whiskers and got away with it. I could at least see the world around but the tigress was blinded for the time being. The jackal continued ingratiatingly, "If you cannot discover a reason to be enemies, why don't you consider being friends? How grand you could make it if you joined forces—you could become supreme in this jungle and the next and the next; no one will ever try to stand up to you, except a crazy tusker, whom you could toss about between you two . . . If you combined you could make all the jungle shake."

His words sounded agreeable. I felt a sudden compassion for my adversary and also gratitude for being spared my life. I struggled to get up on my feet and, mistaking my action, the jackal swiftly withdrew and disappeared before I could say, "You have advised us well." I limped along to the tigress very cautiously and expressed my contrition and desire to make amends. She was in no condition to rise or see me. I cleaned up the bloody mess covering her eyes and sat beside her huge body, paying all attention and performing many acts of tenderness—till she was able to open one eye slightly and stir, and it filled me with dread lest she should kill me instantly. She could have easily done it, if she was so disposed. But a change had come over her too. My ministrations seemed to have helped her recover her breath, vision, and the use of her limbs. She followed me quietly, although both of us were limping, to an adjacent pond and we splashed about in the water till we were cleansed of blood and felt revived.

We have no reckoning of time in the manner of human beings. But by the time the scars on our backs were dry, a litter of four was added to our family. 🐾

Tigers will cup their tongues to lap water up into their mouths.

Marking territory by scraping is a means of communicating as well as of claw-cleaning.

A tree, once chosen, is used repeatedly, and large tigers score deep, longitudinal cuts into the bark.

Tigers depend on their eyes and ears to locate prey.

EXCERPTED FROM A *NATIONAL GEOGRAPHIC* ARTICLE BY

STANLEY BREEDEN

SNARL

WE SET OFF AT SUNRISE ON this winter morning in central India, once again riding Pawan Mala, an old and venerable elephant. Out on the meadows the swamp deer stags are rutting. A tiger roars in the distance, a good omen.

Mahavir, the mahout, steers the elephant toward the tiger's stirring sound. We soon find fresh tiger footprints along a sandy ravine, or nullah—the broad strong pugs of a male. They lead us into dense forest.

We are on the right track; we can smell where the tiger has sprayed a bush to mark his territory. Belinda, my wife, sees the tiger first, an awesome vision in fiery orange and black stripes gliding through the green bamboo tracery. Ignoring us, he walks on and on. We are alongside him now, about thirty feet dis-

tant. Once or twice he glances at us and snarls, pale yellow-green eyes burning.

Suddenly the tiger stops in his tracks. He sees a herd of spotted deer browsing on bamboo at the edge of a small clearing. He makes not a motion—no tail twitch, no ear movement, not even a whisker quivers. He is frozen in the partial cover of a small patch of grass. As long as he is motionless, the deer cannot see him, even at thirty or forty feet. There is no breeze, so they cannot scent him.

Slowly the tiger lies down. For half an hour or more he watches the deer. Then, carefully placing one foot in front of the other so as not to make a sound in the dry leaf litter, he insinuates himself from bush to bush. Closer and closer he moves. It seems our hearts have stopped beating.

The tiger's loudest and most stirring call is his resonant aroom! *which can be heard through the jungle for up to a mile. It is sometimes used as a warning to other tigers.*

Though grazing quietly, the deer are alert. Some does are especially watchful. One sniffs the air; there must be a faint tiger scent, for the doe stamps a forefoot, a sign of mild alarm. The others look up.

The tiger is rigid in a crouch, powerful hind feet gathered under him. The doe stamps her front foot again, raises her tail, gives her bell-like alarm call. The tiger bursts from cover, tail erect, ears forward. In unbelievably fast bounds he rushes the deer. They scatter. . . .

He misses, snarls, and utters a series of moaning roars. Then he rests, lying in a pool of sunlight. We go closer, to be greeted with a snarl and a low, rumbling growl. Never before or since have we seen a tiger with such a bad disposition. We name the tigers we study. This one is Snarl.

Pawan Mala is tired after her long hike. She fidgets, letting us know it is time to return to camp. "Camp" is, in fact, a two-room cabin deep in the forests and bamboo jungles of Kanha National Park. It is an idyllic spot, far from India's crowded cities and towns. . . .

A few days after we meet Snarl, we have a reunion with Arjuna, an old tiger friend, who is on a kill. He is as benevolent as ever. Small scavenging birds and a mongoose nibble at his sambar deer kill. Arjuna is not as tall at the shoulder as Snarl (whom we had seen about three miles away) but is much bulkier, broader in the shoulder. He oozes power, where Snarl is all athleticism.

That evening at dusk we sit on the veranda of our cabin listening to the calls of owls, stone curlews, and nightjars. A distant bark of alarm from a sambar suggests a tiger on the prowl.

Suddenly an unearthly sound that shakes the forest brings Belinda and me out of our chairs. The back of my neck prickles. All other sounds cease. These are the full-throated roars of two tigers in a life-and-death fight. For about ten minutes the roars continue. Then . . . quiet.

The terrible sound had come from the direction of Arjuna and his kill. The next day we set out in the predawn chill. We find Arjuna, still with his sambar—but he is a much changed tiger. A huge swath of skin and flesh has been ripped away between his eyes and down his nose. Constantly he wipes a forepaw across it. We search for the other contestant. A mile distant we come upon Snarl, sitting in a thick patch of undergrowth. He bears a few slight wounds on his shoulder and on the inside of one of his front legs. He snarls at us, eyes burning.

Three months later Arjuna is found dead about eight miles away. His face had festered; unable to hunt, he had died. Snarl takes over his territory.

One day we sight a tigress and her three cubs under a beautiful kulu tree, its white sculptured bark a marvelous contrast to the surrounding black rocks. So we call her Kulu.

It is May and hot, 105°F in the shade. Kulu has dragged her kill, a spotted deer stag, to a cool and protected place—a rock pool surrounded by bamboo. In the early morning all four tigers are crammed into the small water hole. Their coats, sleek and glossy, shine in the sunlight.

After a few minutes Kulu gets up, walks up a small rise, and lies down in the shade. First one cub, then another and another, joins her, rubbing faces or rubbing the whole length of their bodies under her chin. She rubs faces in return and licks them.

Later that day we are out searching for tigers in the heart of Snarl's territory and pause where a few pools of clear water remain deep in a cool forest. We are about three miles from the place where Kulu usually lives with her cubs. We are astonished to find her sitting beside a tiny pool in the bed of a steep-sided stream. What is she doing here? Why has she left her cubs?

Kulu is restless and preoccupied. Normally she would lie asleep in the water or on her back in the sand. But she keeps looking down the nullah, lashing her tail incessantly. Occasionally she moans softly.

Suddenly she sits up, pricks her ears, and stares down the nullah. We follow her gaze. A magnificent male tiger, lean, lithe, and powerful, slowly walks along the streambed. Within about twenty feet of Kulu, he flops down in the sand. It is Snarl. . . .

This is no casual meeting. The easy familiarity between the two is quite evident. Kulu no longer lashes her tail. She lies down full-length in the sand. Snarl lies with his head held regally high.

Kulu snoozes. Then she gets up, yawns widely, stretches. Head low, she walks over to Snarl, who purrs in pleasure and friendship. They touch faces. The tigress lies down with all four feet under her, head on the sand. As darkness falls, Snarl gets up, walks over to Kulu, and straddles her.

They mate. Snarl bites her neck roughly and growls.

Kulu turns her head, curls her lips, and roars right into his face. He roars back. Snarl walks a few paces and flops down again. Kulu rolls sensually onto her back. It is almost dark.

We wonder why Kulu would mate when she already has eight-month-old cubs. They will be with her another thirteen to fifteen months. If she conceives, a new litter will be born in about 3 1/2 months. No tiger in the wild could possibly look after two litters. This mating, then, is most unusual.

A month passes. We see Kulu and her cubs regularly, Snarl occasionally. One morning after a heavy downpour we find the tracks of Kulu and her cubs—but also those of Snarl. They converge in a sandy nullah not far from where the pair had mated. There are signs of a struggle, spots of blood.

As we round a bend, Snarl sneaks out of a bamboo clump just ahead. Where he emerged, we find the remains of the male cub. Deep punctures in his throat show he died a violent death. Part of his hindquarters have been eaten. Snarl has killed again.

We have not long to mourn the cub. A tiger roars nearby, and moments later Kulu appears. Briefly she sniffs her dead cub, then raises her head and roars loudly—a sound unlike any we have ever heard. She turns and is quickly joined by her remaining two cubs.

They walk so close to her that she almost trips over them. The trio disappears into thick bamboo. 🐾

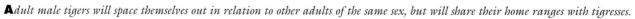

Adult male tigers will space themselves out in relation to other adults of the same sex, but will share their home ranges with tigresses.

Though tigers do have favorite prey species, notably swamp deer, chital, and wild pig, necessity can compel them to subsist on such lowly fare as fish and frogs.

A *tiger needs twelve to fifteen pounds of meat daily.*

T*he tiger uses its rasping tongue not only to groom its fur, but to clean the flesh from its victim's bones.*

AN ORIGINAL ESSAY BY

ART WOLFE

PORTRAIT OF A TIGER

FROM AN ARTIST'S POINT of view, the tiger is the quintessence of a photographic subject—nature's blessings of design. I take every opportunity I can to photograph the tiger. To emphasize the linear symmetry of the regal countenance of these great cats I like to zoom in close and get as tight a portrait of their faces as allowable.

An icon of power, the tiger not only exemplifies strength and cunning, but grace and fluidity of movement. A master at stealth, its intricately striped markings are a sharp contrast against its rich burnt orange and reddish orange coat colorings. With facial stripes as individual as fingerprints, each tiger's portrait is unique.

The compelling beauty of these magnificent animals has more than once totally absorbed me in my work; focusing my attention through the lens of my camera not only on their image, but on their very essence. When I decided I wanted to do a book on the wild cats of the world, the tiger, naturally, was to be one of the main characters. The list of species I targeted for this project would require a superhuman effort or at least a small troop of photographers to secure, and our shooting schedule was very tight. I did not have the luxury of traveling to India or to Russia to try and photograph the tigers in the wild. As a wildlife and nature photographer, I am painfully aware of the endangered status of the tiger. Today, sightings of tigers in their natural habitat are rare events. Nevertheless, even working with captive tigers I managed to experience firsthand the noble majesty of these incredible animals and photograph a great breadth of portraits.

The tiger neither roars nor makes any sound during an attack.

The most memorable of my encounters brought home to me, in a terrifying instant, the cunning and agility of the tiger as hunter, a hunter that pays attention to the eyes of its prey, a hunter that attacks its prey not from the front, but because of some primordial instinct, from behind.

I was photographing a Siberian tiger and had set up my camera fairly close to his enclosure. As I do with many of my subjects, I assured the creature in a low, confident voice that I was not there to threaten or hurt him in any way. He remained docile and seemingly uninterested in my presence and activity, defiantly nonchalant. I shot off several rolls of film without getting so much as a yawn from him; he seemed content to languish in a patch of tall grass several yards away. But the instant I turned my back on him to replenish my supply of film, in just the breadth of the moment that it took me to grab a roll, he was almost literally upon me. Only the barrier between us saved me from becoming an unwitting afternoon snack. The near disaster shook me deeply and reinforced my already great respect for the deadly claws and elongated teeth of this, the most powerful land mammal on earth. Recovering from my fright, I remembered having read that loggers and field workers in tiger habitats wear masks on the back of their heads so that at no time will their back sides be exposed to the tigers around them. Perhaps this technique would be useful for photographers also!

The tiger's aggressive and cunning nature is but one side of his portrait. There is another, a more gentle, nurturing side that my lens captured on another occasion while photographing for my book. Rather than being shaken to my roots witnessing the tiger as hunter, this time I was able to enjoy the more playful side of the cat. I was photographing a mother tiger and her two yearling cubs. The agility and playfulness of the cubs was delightful to watch. The scene was no different than watching two kittens at play—their boundless energy, their instincts, their nuances of behavior—only their great size distinguished them from their domestic cousins. In an hour of photographing them, the cubs never slowed down. Their mother oversaw their antics from a short distance until they stalked and pounced upon her, and she swatted at them with firm gentleness. She tolerated their playful abuse patiently and played the tender and doting mother however rambunctious their behavior became. Through the lens of my camera I watched them, pattern on pattern, a kaleidoscope of stripes and color. They were the very image of life and energy.

But one of my most remarkable images is that of a Bengal tiger. Photographically, it was an ideal situation for shooting. It was late afternoon light, and I was able to get in fairly close to the tiger. Its eyes were penetrating, and in this particular setting with the afternoon sun directly behind me, the effect the light had on the cat's eyes when it looked straight into the camera was mesmerizing. When the color of its eyes flashed golden amber, the eyes seemed not only to be looking at me, but right through me. I felt like I was photographing an apparition; the ghostly impression of the species. Riveted by his gaze and by his image, I stared through the lens and, with a trip of the shutter, I felt I had captured the portrait of the last tiger on earth. 🐾

A *tiger's facial stripes are as individual as fingerprints and aid in identification.*

A *tiger will not mate for life but will mate with selected females for a number of seasons.*

THE KILL

BEYOND THE FACT THAT HE was born in a ravine running deep into the foothills and was one of a family of three, I know nothing of his early history.

He was about a year old when, attracted by the calling of a chital hind early one November morning, I found his pugmarks in the sandy bed of a little stream known locally as Pipal Pani. I thought at first that he had strayed from his mother's care, but, as week succeeded week and his single tracks showed on the game paths of the forest, I came to the conclusion that the near approach of the breeding season was an all-sufficient reason for his being alone. Jealously guarded one day, protected at the cost of the parent life if necessary, and set adrift the next is the lot of all jungle folk; nature's method of preventing inbreeding.

That winter he lived on peafowl, kakar, small pig, and an occasional chital hind, making his home in a prostrate giant of the forest felled for no apparent reason, and hollowed out by time and porcupines. Here he brought most of his kills, basking, when the days were cold, on the smooth bole of the tree, where many a leopard had basked before him.

It was not until January was well advanced that I saw the cub at close quarters. I was out one evening without any definite object in view, when I saw a crow rise from the ground and wipe its beak as it lit on the branch of a tree. Crows, vultures, and magpies always interest me in the jungle, and many are the kills I have found both in India and in Africa with the help of these

Territory is important to tigers. Adult males face the greatest risk in mortality because they fight for feeding and hunting grounds and for mating rights with females.

birds. On the present occasion the crow led me to the scene of an overnight tragedy. A chital had been killed and partly eaten and, attracted to the spot probably as I had been, a party of men passing along the road, distant some fifty yards, had cut up and removed the remains. All that was left of the chital were a few splinters of bone and a little congealed blood off which the crow had lately made his meal. The absence of thick cover and the proximity of the road convinced me that the animal responsible for the kill had not witnessed the removal and that it would return in due course; so I decided to sit up, and made myself as comfortable in a plum tree as the thorns permitted.

I make no apology to you, my reader, if you differ with me on the ethics of the much-debated subject of sitting up over kills. Some of my most pleasant shikar memories center round the hour or two before sunset that I have spent in a tree over a natural kill, ranging from the time when, armed with a muzzle-loader whipped round with brass wire to prevent the cracked barrel from bursting, I sat over a langur killed by a leopard, to a few days ago, when with the most modern rifle across my knees, I watched a tigress and her two full-grown cubs eat up the sambur stag they had killed, and counted myself no poorer for not having secured a trophy.

True, on the present occasion there is no kill below me, but, for the reasons given, that will not affect my chance of a shot; scent to interest the jungle folk there is in plenty in the blood-soaked ground, as witness the old gray-whiskered boar who has been quietly rooting along for the past ten minutes, and who suddenly stiffens to attention as he comes into the line of the blood-tainted wind. His snout held high, and worked as only a pig can work that member, tells him more than I was able to glean from the ground which showed no tracks; his method of approach, a short excursion to the right and back into the wind, and then a short excursion to the left and again back into the wind, each manoeuver bringing him a few yards nearer, indicates the chital was killed by a tiger. Making sure once and again that nothing worth eating has been left, he finally trots off and disappears from view.

Two chital, both with horns in velvet, now appear and from the fact that they are coming down-wind, and making straight for the blood-soaked spot, it is evident they were witnesses to the overnight tragedy. Alternately snuffing the ground, or standing rigid with every muscle tensed for instant flight, they satisfy their curiosity and return the way they came.

Curiosity is not a human monopoly: many an animal's life is cut short by indulging in it. A dog leaves the verandah to bark at a shadow, a deer leaves the herd to investigate a tuft of grass that no wind agitated, and the waiting leopard is provided with a meal.

The sun is nearing the winter line when a movement to the right front attracts attention. An animal has crossed an opening between two bushes at the far end of a wedge of scrub bushes at my end part, and out into the open, with never a look to right or left, steps the cub. Straight up to the spot where his kill had been he goes, his look of expectancy giving place to one of disappointment as he realizes that his chital, killed, possibly, after hours of patient stalking, is gone. The splinters of bone and congealed blood are rejected, and his interest centers on a tree stump lately used as a butcher's block, to which some shreds of flesh are adhering. I was not the only one who carried firearms in these jungles and, if the cub was to grow into a tiger, it was necessary he should be taught the danger of carelessly approaching kills in daylight. A scatter-gun and dust-shot would have served my purpose better, but the rifle will have to do this time; and, as he raises his head to smell the stump, my bullet crashes into the hard wood an inch from his nose. Only once in the years that followed did the cub forget that lesson.

The following winter I saw him several times. His ears did not look so big now and he had changed his baby hair for a coat of rich tawny red with well-defined stripes. The hollow tree had been given up to its rightful owners, a pair of leopards, new quarters found in a thick belt of scrub skirting the foothills, and young sambar added to his menu.

On my annual descent from the hills next winter, the familiar pugmarks no longer showed on the game paths and at the drinking places, and for several weeks I thought the cub had abandoned his old haunts and gone further afield. Then one morning his absence was explained, for side by side with his tracks were the smaller and more elongated tracks of the mate he had gone to find. I only once saw the tigers, for the cub was a tiger now, together. I had been out before dawn to try to bag a serow that lived on the foothills, and returning along a fire track my attention was arrested by a vulture, perched on the dead limb of a sal tree.

The bird had his back towards me and was facing a short stretch of scrub with dense jungle beyond. Dew was still heavy on the ground, and without a sound I reached the tree and peered round. One antler of a dead sambar, for no living deer would lie in that position, projected above the low bushes. A convenient moss-covered rock afforded my rubber-shod feet silent and safe hold, and as I drew myself erect, the sambar came into full view. The hind quarters had been eaten away and, lying on either side of the kill, were the pair, the tiger being on the far side with only his hind legs showing. Both tigers were asleep. Ten feet straight in front, to avoid a dead branch, and thirty feet to the left would give me a shot at the tiger's neck, but in planning the stalk I had forgotten the silent spectator. Where I stood I was invisible to him, but before the ten feet had been covered I came into view and, alarmed at my near proximity, he flapped off his perch, omitting as he did so to notice a thin creeper dependent from a branch above him against which he collided, and came ignominiously to ground. The tigress was up and away in an instant, clearing at a bound the kill and her mate, the tiger not being slow to follow; a possible shot, but too risky with thick jungle ahead where a wounded animal would have all the advantages. To those who have never tried it, I can recommend the stalking of leopards and tigers on their kills as a most pleasant form of sport. Great care should however be taken over the shot, for if the animal is not killed outright, or anchored, trouble is bound to follow.

A week later the tiger resumed his bachelor existence. A change had now come over his nature. Hitherto he had not objected to my visiting his kills but, after his mate left, at the first drag I followed up I was given very clearly to understand that no liberties would in future be permitted. The angry growl of a tiger at close quarters, than which there is no more terrifying sound in the jungles, has to be heard to be appreciated.

Early in March the tiger killed his first full-grown buffalo. I was near the foothills one evening when the agonized bellowing of a buffalo, mingled with the angry roar of a tiger, rang through the forest. I located the sound as coming from a ravine about six hundred yards away. The going was bad, mostly over loose rocks and through thorn bushes, and when I crawled up a steep bluff commanding a view of the ravine the buffalo's struggles were over, and the tiger was nowhere to be seen. For an hour I lay with finger on trigger without seeing anything of the tiger. At dawn next morning I again crawled up the bluff, to find the buffalo lying just as I had left her. The soft ground, torn up by hoof and claw, testified to the desperate nature of the struggle, and it was not until the buffalo had been hamstrung that the tiger had finally succeeded in pulling her down, in a fight which had lasted from ten to fifteen minutes. The tiger's tracks led across the ravine and, on following them up, I found a long smear of blood on a rock, and, a hundred yards further on, another smear on a fallen tree. The wound inflicted by the buffalo's horns was in the tiger's head and sufficiently severe to make the tiger lose all interest in the kill, for he never returned to it.

Three years later the tiger, disregarding the lesson received when a cub (his excuse may have been that it was the close season for tigers), incautiously returned to a kill, over which a zamindar and some of his tenants were sitting at night, and received a bullet in the shoulder which fractured the bone. No attempt was made to follow him up, and thirty-six hours later, his shoulder covered with a swarm of flies, he limped through the compound of the inspection bungalow, crossed a bridge flanked on the far side by a double row of tenanted houses, the occupants of which stood at their doors to watch him pass, entered the gate of a walled-in compound and took possession of a vacant godown. Twenty-four hours later, possibly alarmed by the number of people who had collected from neighboring villages to see him, he left the compound the way he had entered it, passed our gate, and made his way to the lower end of our village. A bullock belonging to one of our tenants had died the previous night and had been dragged into some bushes at the edge of the village; this the tiger found, and here he remained a few days, quenching his thirst at an irrigation furrow.

When we came down from the hills two months later the tiger was living on small animals (calves, sheep, goats, etc.) that he was able to catch on the outskirts of the village. By March his wound had healed, leaving his right foot turned inwards. Returning to the forest where he had been wounded, he levied heavy toll on the village cattle, taking, for safety's sake, but one meal off each and in this way killing five times as many as he would ordinarily have done. The zamindar who had wounded him and who had a herd of some four hundred head of cows and buffaloes was the chief sufferer.

In the succeeding years he gained as much in size as in reputation, and many were the attempts made by sportsmen, and others, to bag him.

One November evening, a villager, armed with a single-barrel muzzle-loading gun, set out to try to bag a pig, selecting for his ground machan an isolated bush growing in a twenty-yard-wide *rowkah* (dry watercourse) running down the center of some broken ground. This ground was rectangular, flanked on the long sides by cultivated land and on the short sides by a road, and by a ten-foot canal that formed the boundary between our cultivation and the forest. In front of the man was a four-foot-high bank with a cattle track running along the upper edge; behind him a patch of dense scrub. At 8 P.M. an animal appeared on the track and, taking what aim he could, he fired. On receiving the shot the animal fell off the bank, and passed within a few feet of the man, grunting as it entered the scrub behind. Casting aside his blanket, the man ran to his hut two hundred yards away. Neighbors soon collected and, on hearing the man's account, came to the conclusion that a pig had been hard hit. It would be a pity, they said, to leave the pig for hyenas and jackals to eat, so a lantern was lit and as a party of six bold spirits set out to retrieve the bag, one of my tenants (who declined to join the expedition, and who confessed to me later that he had no stomach for looking for wounded pig in dense scrub in the dark) suggested that the gun should be loaded and taken.

His suggestion was accepted and, as a liberal charge of powder was being rammed home, the wooden ramrod jammed and broke inside the barrel. A trivial accident which undoubtedly saved the lives of six men. The broken rod was eventually and after great trouble extracted, the gun loaded, and the party set off.

Arrived at the spot where the animal had entered the bushes, a careful search was made and, on blood being found,

every effort to find the "pig" was made; it was not until the whole area had been combed out that the quest for that night was finally abandoned. Early next morning the search was resumed, with the addition of my informant of weak stomach, who was a better woodsman than his companions and who, examining the ground under a bush where there was a lot of blood, collected and brought some bloodstained hairs to me, which I recognized as tiger's hairs. A brother sportsman was with me for the day and together we went to have a look at the ground.

The reconstruction of jungle events from signs on the ground has always held great interest for me. True, one's deductions are sometimes wrong, but they are also sometimes right. In the present instance I was right in placing the wound in the inner forearm of the right foreleg, but was wrong in assuming the leg had been broken and that the tiger was a young animal and a stranger to the locality.

There was no blood beyond the point where the hairs had been found and, as tracking on the hard ground was impossible, I crossed the canal to where the cattle track ran through a bed of sand. Here from the pugmarks I found that the wounded animal was not a young tiger as I had assumed, but my old friend the Pipal Pani tiger, who, when taking a shortcut through the village, had in the dark been mistaken for a pig.

Once before when badly wounded he had passed through the settlement without harming man or beast, but he was older now, and if driven by pain and hunger might do considerable damage. A disconcerting prospect, for the locality was thickly populated, and I was due to leave within the week, to keep an engagement that could not be put off.

For three days I searched every bit of the jungle between the canal and the foothills, an area of about four square miles, without finding any trace of the tiger. On the fourth afternoon, as I was setting out to continue the search, I met an old woman and her son hurriedly leaving the jungle. From them I learnt that the tiger was calling near the foothills and that all the cattle in the jungle had stampeded. When out with a rifle I invariably go alone; it is safer in a mix-up, and one can get through the jungle more silently. However, I stretched a point on this occasion, and let the boy accompany me, since he was very keen on showing me where he had heard the tiger.

Arrived at the foothills, the boy pointed to a dense bit of cover, bounded on the far side by the fire track to which I have already referred, and on the near side by the Pipal Pani stream. Running parallel to and about a hundred yards from the stream was a shallow depression some twenty feet wide, more or less open on my side and fringed with bushes on the side nearer the stream. A well-used path crossed the depression at right angles. Twenty yards from the path, and on the open side of the depression, was a small tree. If the tiger came down the path he would in all like-lihood stand for a shot on clearing the bushes. Here I decided to take my stand and, putting the boy into the tree with his feet on a level with my head and instructing him to signal with his toes if from his raised position he saw the tiger before I did, I put my back to the tree and called.

You who have spent as many years in the jungle as I have need no description of the call of a tigress in search of a mate, and to you less fortunate ones I can only say that the call, to acquire which necessitates close observation and the liberal use of throat salve, cannot be described in words.

To my great relief, for I had crawled through the jungle for three days with finger on trigger, I was immediately answered from a distance of about five hundred yards, and for half an hour thereafter—it may have been less and certainly appeared more—the call was tossed back and forth. On the one side the urgent summons of the king, and on the other, the subdued and coaxing answer of his handmaiden. Twice the boy signaled, but I had as yet seen nothing of the tiger, and it was not until the setting sun was flooding the forest with golden light that he suddenly appeared, coming down the path at a fast walk with never a pause as he cleared the bushes. When halfway across the depression, and just as I was raising the rifle, he turned to the right and came straight towards me.

This manoeuver, unforeseen when selecting my stand, brought him nearer than I had intended he should come and, moreover, presented me with a head shot which at that short range I was not prepared to take. Resorting to an old device, learned long years ago and successfully used on similar occasions, the tiger was brought to a stand without being alarmed. With one paw poised, he slowly raised his head, exposing as he did so his chest and throat. After the impact of the heavy bullet, he struggled to his feet and tore blindly through the forest, coming down with a crash within a few yards of where, attracted by the calling of a chital hind one November morning, I had first seen his pugmarks.

It was only then that I found he had been shot under a misapprehension, for the wound which I feared might make him dangerous proved on examination to be almost healed and caused by a pellet of lead having severed a small vein in his right forearm.

Pleasure at having secured a magnificent trophy—he measured 10'3" over curves and his winter coat was in perfect condition—was not unmixed with regret, for never again would the jungle folk and I listen with held breath to his deep-throated call resounding through the foothills, and never again would his familiar pugmarks show on the game paths that he and I had trodden for fifteen years. 🐾

Tigers are vulnerable to diseases such as rabies and distemper, and to any diseases suffered by their prey.

CONTRIBUTORS

Maurice G. Hornocker is the director of the Hornocker Wildlife Institute at the University of Idaho. A wildlife biologist and one of the world's foremost authorities on the great cats, Hornocker pioneered the use of radio telemetry to conduct field studies of cougars and jaguars. Along with his associate Dr. Howard Quigley, Hornocker is co-director of the Siberian Tiger Project, an international research program based in eastern Russia studying the ecology and range and habitat requirements of the Siberian tiger as a basis for a plan to try to save it from extinction.

Peter Matthiessen is an award-winning novelist, naturalist, short story writer, and essayist. An inveterate world traveler and eminent conservationist, he has been awarded the African Wildlife Leadership Foundation Award and the John Burroughs Medal, as well as the Gold Medal for Distinction in Natural History by the Academy of Natural Sciences, Philadelphia. Matthiessen, the author of more than twenty books, is the founder (with Howard Humes) of *The Paris Review* and, in 1979, won the American Book Award for *The Snow Leopard*.

Geoffrey Ward is a renowned historian, author, and screenwriter who spent his boyhood in India and wrote of his later return to the Indian jungles. He authored *Tiger-Wallahs—Encounters with the Men Who Tried to Save the Greatest of the Great Cats*, a tribute to some of the men who have dedicated their lives to protecting and preserving the world's remaining tigers. Ward has served as writer or principal writer for a number of PBS documentaries, including "The Civil War," "Huey Long," "Nixon," "The Kennedys," "Baseball," and "The West." His books include *American Originals, Before the Trumpet, A First-Class Temperament,* and (with Ric and Ken Burns) the bestselling *The Civil War: An Illustrated History*.

Elizabeth C. Reed was a contributing writer to *National Geographic* and a veteran foster mother to countless zoo babies toted home by her husband, Dr. Theodore H. Reed, one-time director of the Smithsonian Institution's National Zoological Park in Washington, D.C. From hybrid bears and grizzlies to leopards and lemurs and tigers, Reed wrote about her many years of family adventures hand-raising members of some of the world's endangered species.

Col. A. N. W. Powell was a big game hunter in India during an era when tigers were hunted for sport. He was the author of *Call of the Tiger*, a collection of stories about the animals and jungle that he loved. The book culminates in his mastery of the art of calling up a tiger.

R. K. Narayan is the author of numerous books including the dozen volumes of his Novels of Malgudi series. His other writings include his memoirs, travel diaries, essay collections, and three anthologies of Indian legends.

Stanley Breeden is a veteran wildlife photographer and writer for *National Geographic*. Breeden has been known to photograph tigers from atop an elephant, using an eleven-foot tripod to steady his camera, in India's Kanha National Park. His noteworthy television documentary "Land of the Tiger" was first broadcast in 1985.

Art Wolfe is a world-renowned nature photographer and advocate, artist, teacher, and documentarian. He has authored more than twenty books and for two seasons hosted ESPN's *American Photo's Safari*. Wolfe produces a biannual multimedia fund-raising program for AIDS and cancer research, which also benefits the Woodland Park Zoo, and is a member of the Advisory Board of the Wildlife Conservation Society.

Maj. Jim Corbett was perhaps India's first conservationist. Through his work for the district officials of Kumaon, Corbett was known to rural villagers across India and Africa as their protector against tigers that had become man-eaters. He authored the book *Man-Eaters of Kumaon*.

PHOTOGRAPHERS

Peter Arnold, Inc., New York: pp. 10, 38-39, 44 © Gerald Lacz; pp. 86-87 © Fateh Singh Rathore

Erwin and Peggy Bauer, Livingston, Montana: pp. 4-5 (Bengal), 7, 27 (Siberian), 51, 60-61 (Siberian), 62 (Siberian), 63, 72 (Siberian), 73 (Siberian), 96, backcover screen (Siberian)

Dan Blackburn, Los Angeles, California: pp. 52-53

John Botkin, Pine, Colorado: pp. 6 (Bengal), 7, 11, 16 (Bengal), 19 (Bengal), 24-25, 30 (Bengal), 31 (Siberian), 33, 37 (Bengal), 40, 41, 45, 55 (Bengal), 64-65, 67 (Bengal), 76 (Bengal), 77 (Bengal), 89 (Bengal), 95, 99 (Bengal), 109 (Bengal)

Davis/Lynn Images (Tim Davis/Renee Lynn), Santa Fe, New Mexico: pp. 20-21, 22-23, 34-35, 50 (Bengal & Siberian), 58-59, 84 (Bengal), 85 (Bengal), 88 (Bengal), 108 (Bengal), 110-111

Michael H. Francis, Billings, Montana: p. 1 (Siberian)

Tom and Pat Leeson, Vancouver, Washington: pp. 12-13, 46-47, 56-57, 66 (Siberian), 68-69 (Siberian), 74-75 (Siberian), 82 (Siberian), 116-117 (Siberian), 118 (Sumatran), 119 (Siberian)

Charles and Rita Summers, Parker, Colorado: pp. 14-15 (Siberian), 18, 26 (Siberian), 28-29 (Siberian), 32 (Siberian), 42-43 (Siberian), 54, 70-71, 80-81, 83 (Siberian), 90-91, 92-93 (Siberian), 94, 112-113, 114-115

Art Wolfe, Seattle, Washington: pp. 2-3 (Bengal), 49 (Indochinese), 97 (Bengal), 98 (Bengal), 101, 102-103, 104 (Bengal), 105, 106-107 (Bengal), Cover (Bengal), Backcover screen

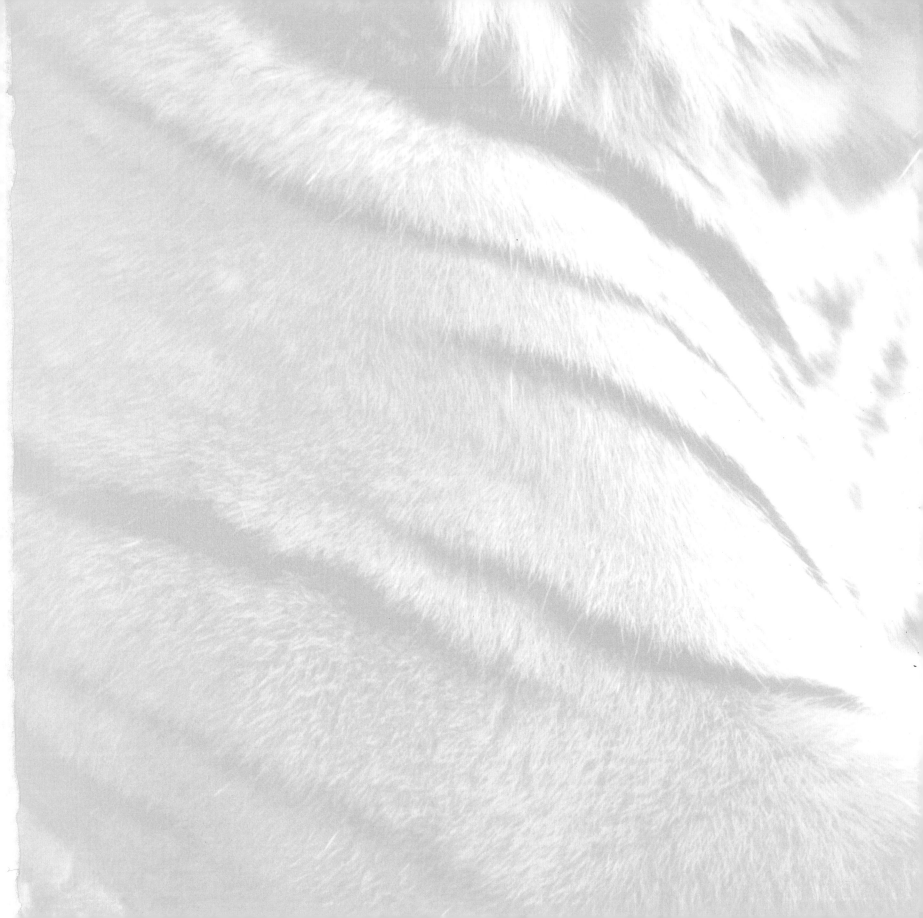